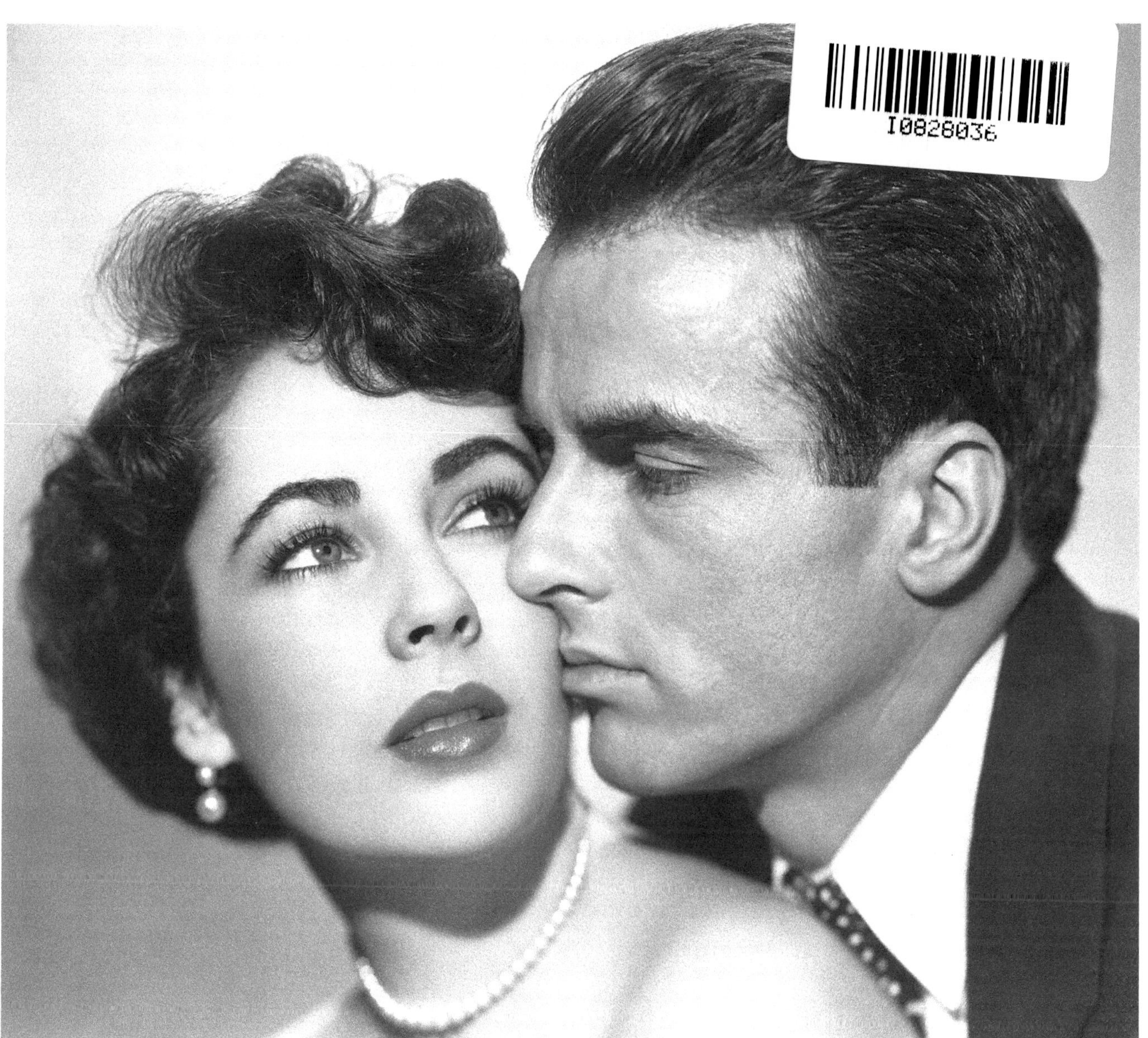

They Did It With Their Clothes On

by TOM CULVER

THEY DID IT WITH THEIR CLOTHES ON

Published by TVGuestpert Publishing

ISBN-13: 978-1-7358981-9-3
BISAC CODES: PER004000, PER004010, PER004050
Nationwide Distribution through Ingram

Front Book Cover Design: Tanja Prokop
Book Design: Carole Allen Design Studio
Author Headshots: Michael Helms
Reviewed by: Al Dell'Aglio
Movie photos licensed through Getty Images by Author.
This book was not written by AI.

Edited by TVGuestpert Publishing
11664 National Blvd, #345
Los Angeles, CA. 90064
310-584-1504
www.TVGuestpertPublishing.com
www.TVGuestpert.com
First Printing 2023
10 9 8 7 6 5 4 3 2 1

Acknowledgements

I HAD NO IDEA what writing a book entailed, especially when dealing with rights to photographs! Many thanks to Getty Images.

I want to thank Bonita Mann, Jean Louis Delezane, and Mary Still for their endless work and dedication. All of them are professionals who made this book happen.

And thanks to the publisher, Jacquie Jordan and her group at TVGuestpert Publishing, who took notes and photos and made it into a book! I'm an avid reader and I always thought that books were a living thing. They've always been very important to me.

Thanks to everyone who helped make this book come to fruition.

— *Tom Culver*

Table of Contents

Foreword

I've been a costume designer now for fifty-four years, Emeritus President of the Costume Designers Guild, Emmy Award winner, Film and TV costume designer, Opera costume designer, Creative Director for Film and Television Costume Design, and creator of "Storytelling for Camera through Costumes," starting in Fall '24 at the Lucas Film School at USC.

I met Tom in 1978 at Western Costume Company when it was located on Melrose Avenue, adjacent to Paramount Pictures in Los Angeles. He had a room on the mezzanine floor where he worked with the costume designers he was assigned to and the costume designers who requested him. I was the first one; then, forever after, the other.

Tom would take me to the upper floors of Western Costume where few ventured. The 7th floor was jewelry, where exotic custom pieces resided, rarely rented, under layers of dust, and the very scary 5th floor dedicated to furs. When the doors of the elevator opened and you heard a tiny chorus of life singing amongst the pelts and minks, you prayed the doors would close faster and deliver you to a safer floor.

Although I had a classical costume design education and seven years' experience as a designer in many forms of theatre, some films, and commercials on the East coast, I was a Hollywood neophyte. Tom was not.

He provided a great deal of guidance and not a few laughs. One time he hugged me so hard he unsnapped my bra, to his everlasting delight! Tom is a fan of glamour, a connoisseur of allure and a victim of the steam of the "hot" scene. These are his credentials as an expert in the world he opens to us in *They Did It with Their Clothes On*.

In the 1950s, at my house, SEX was a four-letter word. But every Saturday, at the theater, we watched romantic couples, wearing brilliantly designed costumes, come close to losing themselves in each other only to cut to waves, skies or operas symbolizing lovemaking.

This symbolism was very unhelpful in my first forays into intimacy but once I became knowledgeable in the mechanics, those images provided (and still provide) much enjoyment for the imaginative aspect of the event.

Tom is devoted to titillation and will tell you some fabulous stories throughout this book. *They Did it with Their Clothes On* speaks to me. Just read and listen to his voice. Seductive.

Thank you, Tom.

Jacqueline SaintAnne
At the Totality of the Solar Eclipse
April 8th, 2024

Introduction

A few months ago, a friend and I had just come out of a movie theatre. We'd just seen an important new film and it was about as subtle as World War II. Nothing left to the imagination!

We laughed and I said, "Oh, for the good old days. Those films had class and style. They did it with their clothes on."

Before I pulled up into my driveway, I was making a mental note of the great, near great, and merely wonderful movies with beautiful, seductive scenes. Some subtle, some steamy. But they all "did it with their clothes on."

This book is dedicated to movie memories of another time when seduction was only implied and that was enough! We were allowed to use our imaginations!

Making love on the silver screen was subtle. Simple things told us love was made, such as a fluttering curtain, a record player with the needle stuck in the last groove and no one cared to fix it. Or the next morning we'd see a pot of coffee boiling and she'd have on his pajama top. This was daring and wonderful.

Nor was seduction always sexual. Some performers hit the screen and literally tickled your senses. Well, here's to having your senses tickled, and stroked, and being seduced by a lot of people whom you've only met on the silver screen!

— *Tom*

HELL'S ANGELS

Starring Jean Harlow & Ben Lyons

The scene opens at a big party during World War I. Jean asks her boyfriend's brother to drive her home. He does. She asks him up for a nightcap. He accepts and it's all over for him.

She pours them a drink and utters the famous lines, "Would you be shocked if I put on something more comfortable?" She did, and he was!

He is getting very uncomfortable. After all, it's his brother's girlfriend.

You can almost see the steam coming out of his collar. He stands up in a last-ditch effort to leave. She says, "Pull me up". He pulls her up and they kiss; we cut to her boyfriend back at the barracks in bed, looking at his watch, wondering where his brother is.

Not only did Jean Harlow slip into something comfortable but she slipped into a lot of minds. And a funny thing, women liked her, too. This dazzling blonde with pencil thin eyebrows, big blue mascaraed eyes, and a body that was only sensational.

She was brassy-sassy and very available on that big silver screen.

This WWI epic had its long-awaited premiere at the Grauman Theatre in Hollywood on May 27th, 1930. Hollywood Boulevard was shut down for several blocks East and West of Highland and mock airplanes were hanging between the theatre and the Hollywood Roosevelt Hotel, just across the street from the theatre. A massive crowd was in attendance, and they went wild (as the crowd usually does for a blonde) when Jean Harlow was introduced!

Jean Harlow went over to MGM and became a huge star, then dying a sad and senseless death at age twenty-six.

Designer Howard Greer is not listed in the film credits, but costume books all credit him as the Costume Designer.

RKO-1930

Black & White and some Technicolor Footage

Director-Howard Hughes

Costume Design-Howard Greer

RED DUST

WHAT ELSE DO YOU DO BESIDES WORK?

DON'T YOU KNOW ANY GAMES?

Clark Gable as Dennis Carson

Jean Harlow as Vantine

Mary Astor as Barbara Willis

Gene Raymond as Barbara's husband, Gary

In *RED DUST*, Clark Gable comes home from a rough day at the rubber plantation. It's also raining outside. He comes into his combination humble home/office to find Jean Harlow has arrived via boat for a few days and just staying 'til the next boat comes by. (How come that never happens to me?)

> They talk. He's rude. She admires his parrot. He's still rude. She makes him a cheese sandwich. He weakens. He pulls her onto his lap, and we cut back to the parrot in the cage -- looking stunned.

What was the parrot thinking and what were we thinking? They were great together. They deserved each other. Clark was in a virtual supermarket of beautiful women in this film. Mary Astor completed this menage-a-trois.

The film was later remade as *MOGAMBO*, set this time in Africa, with Ava Gardner in the Jean Harlow role, Grace Kelly in the Mary Astor role and Clark Gable reprising himself, and still wielding a lot of sex appeal with a sense of humor.

Metro-Goldwyn-Mayer 1932

Black and White

Producer-Hunt Stromberg

Director-Victor Fleming

Story-John Lee Mahin

Costume Design-Adrian

SHE DONE HIM WRONG

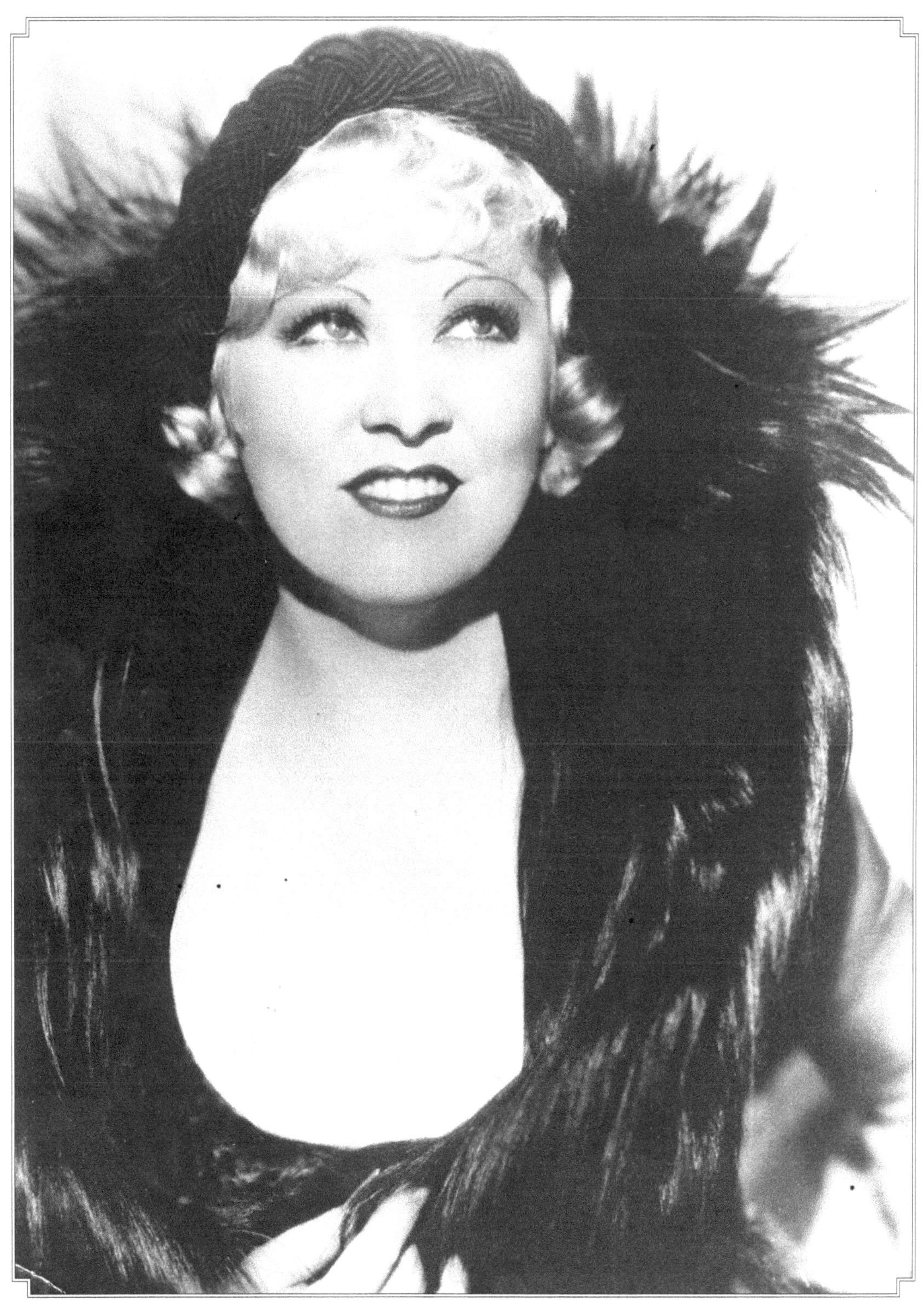

SHE DONE HIM WRONG

WHY DON'T YOU COME UP SOME TIME AND SEE ME?

Mae West as Lady Lou

Cary Grant as Captain Cummings of the Bowery Rescue Mission

Gilbert Roland, Noah Beery Sr., Owen Moore

It's the Gay Nineties! The New York Bowery! The New York Bowery is lusty and brawling. And a lady named Lou is a big part of it. Her previous boyfriend is up the river, the present one is busy running a saloon and literally printing money to keep her in diamonds. She's got her eyes on number three, the handsome Captain Cummings. He's in the saloon often trying to save her soul. (I don't know IF he has that much time!) Lou loves diamonds and wears lots of them.

"Diamonds are part of my career," she tells Gilbert Roland. Mae wrote the script. Actually, it was based on a play that she had written and starred in on Broadway, "Diamond Lil."

She was on the Paramount lot preparing the picture and looking for a leading man when she saw HIM.

"If he can talk, I'll take him," and take him, she did. This was Cary Grant's first major film role.

Mae sang three songs in the film "Easy Rider," "I Like a Guy That Takes His Time," "Frankie and Johnny." Her hair is swept up in beautiful waves. She wears big picture hats and an array of magnificent jewelry. Her gowns were daring! It was said she even moved when she was standing still.

Her films helped save Paramount during the very difficult time of "The Big Crash."

Paramount Pictures-1933

Producer-William LeBaron

Director-Lowell Sherman

Cinematography-Charles Lang

Costume Design-Edith Head

THE GAY DIVORCEE

Fred Astaire as Guy Holden

Ginger Rodgers as Mimi Glossop

This was Fred Astaire's and Ginger Rodgers's second picture together. The first was *FLYING DOWN TO RIO*. In *RIO*, they weren't the stars, but they managed to steal the movie. By the time *RIO* opened in the USA, Fred was in England doing the stage version of *THE GAY DIVORCEE*. Pandro S. Berman went to London to see IF this musical stage play would transfer to film. It could. And so, they did!

The sub-plots keep us busy in this film; but, after all, it isn't the plot that mattered. The brilliant dancing, wonderful songs and the stunning Art Deco sets were more than enough to keep us mesmerized plus a very young Betty Grable was very much in evidence.

It's evening. Fred and Ginger are dressed to the nines. He's in tails. She's in a wonderful gown, form fitting AND oh, what a form!

She's been avoiding him. He's on the prowl, looking for her. He spies her in the supper club. She leaves. He follows her to a beautiful outdoor pavilion. The shutters open at one end to frame this picture. We see the ocean shimmering, the waves breaking.

He talks. She listens.

He sings "Night and Day," and the seduction begins.

She walks away. He reaches for her hand. They dance. She tries to leave. He won't let her. He's made for her. They execute some of the most intricate steps. She raises her skirt, a little like Spanish dancing. She says yes-she says no. She teases. All this is happening in the dance. As they end the dance, he slowly drops her onto a white leather banquette. He brushes his hands together to signify the end and asks "Cigarette?" She nods her head no.

Not only did these wonderfully talented people do it with their clothes on, but they also did it standing up to music!

These two deserve their place in film history-such taste, class, and elegance.

RKO-1934

Black and White

Director-Mark Sandrich

Producer-Pandro S. Berman

Cinematography-David Abel

Art Deco sets-Van Nest Polgalse & Carrol Clark

Costume Design-Walter Plunkett

"Night and Day"-Cole Porter

IT HAPPENED ONE NIGHT

Clark Gable as Peter, a renegade newsman

Claudette Colbert as Ellen Andrews, a renegade heiress

Claudette Colbert has just escaped from her father's boat. He was holding her prisoner because she eloped with a man whom the father thinks is a fortune hunter.

On a bus back to New York, she meets Clark Gable who has just been fired from the newspaper. He is a little hung over and testy, and she's sitting in his seat!

This is the beginning of a unique romance that takes us from Florida to New York via many back roads and motels.

First Motel Stop: It's raining heavily. She's insulted that he expects her to share a room. He's doing it this way to save money. He gives her the choice of beds and strings a rope between them and hangs a blanket over the rope as a divider and this becomes "The Walls of Jericho."

Second Motel Stop: Again, he strings a rope between the beds and hangs a blanket over the rope. They've been through several wonderfully crazy moments and by now, they're obviously falling in love. They are lying in bed. She asks him if he's ever been in love.

Clark says, "I saw an island in the Pacific once. Never been able to forget it. That's where I'd like to take her. She'd have to be the sort of girl who'd, well, jump in the surf and love it as much as I do."

Claudette, feeling romantic, is still on her side of The Walls of Jcricho.

Clark says, "Nights when you, the moon, and the water all become one. You feel you are part of a big and marvelous... That's the only place to live. Why, the stars are so close overhead you feel you can reach up and stir them around."

Claudette is dying to say something. She wants him. She can hardly contain herself.

Clark speaks again, "Certainly I've thought about it. If I could ever find a girl who's hungry for those things."

Claudette appears at the end of the blanket, runs to his side, falls to her knees, and holds him.

She says, "Take me with you, Peter. Take me to your island. I want to do all the things you've talked about."

"You better go back to your bed," he says.

Claudette says, "I love you. Nothing else matters. We can run away. Everything will take care of itself. I can't live without you".

Clark repeats (They're still holding each other), "You'd better go back to your bed."

"I'm sorry." She runs to her bed sobbing and cries herself to sleep. Clark lies awake, thinking, upset.

"Hey, brat. Did you mean that? Would you really go?" He looks over the top of the blanket at her. She's asleep.

Third Motel Stop: Glen Falls, Michigan. Claudette's left her aviator husband at the altar. (This was the church wedding). A getaway car is waiting for her "out back." It's all over… almost.

The elopement is annulled.

We're outside a motel. The owners are discussing the new guests.

Lady: "They made me get them a rope and a blanket. On a night like this. What do you reckon that's for?"

Man: "Danged if I know. I just brung them a trumpet. One of those toy kinds, he sent me to the store to get it."

Lady: "What in the world do they want them for?"

Man: "I don't know."

Trumpet blows and we see The Walls of Jericho fall AND the lights go out!

Columbia Pictures-1934

Black and White

Director-Frank Capra

Script-Robert Riskin

Costume Design-Robert Kalloch

Cinematography-Joseph Walker

THE THIN MAN

OH, NICKY, I LOVE YOU BECAUSE YOU KNOW SUCH LOVELY PEOPLE.

William Powell as Nick Charles

Myrna Loy as Nora Charles

ASTA, their terrier!

This team has never been equaled. (Well, maybe Spencer Tracy and Katharine Hepburn.) They were elegant, charming, witty and she had a lot of money which they both loved to spend. He drank too much, adored her, and loved to walk their dog. Not a bad life for either of them. She was lovely, wore beautiful clothes and even liked his oddball assortment of friends. She was always a lady. They were perfect together and their rapport was delightful! Affectionately insulting but delightful! Of course, in those days in film, even married couples had separate beds.

> They've just solved the case and are on a train headed to California. Having just bid the honeymoon couple good night, they're back in their own compartment with top and bottom berths. Nora is sitting on the bottom berth, starting to undress. Nick is standing up, also undressing.
>
> Nora tells Nick, "Nicky, put Asta in here with me tonight."
>
> "Oh, yeah."
>
> He puts Asta up in the top berth. That was that. Nothing else to be said... or seen. Asta even put his paws over his eyes. No peeking!!

Nick was not the thin man. The murder victim was but the name looked so great on the marquee, MGM kept *THE THIN MAN* as part of the subsequent film titles which totaled six.

Metro-Goldwyn-Mayer-1934

Black and White

Director-W.S. Van Dyke

Novel-Dashiell Hammett

Cinematography-James Wong Howe

Costume Design-Dolly Tree

CAMILLE

In the gay, half-world of Paris, the gentlemen of the day meet the girls of the moment at certain theaters, balls, and gambling clubs where the code was discretion. But the game was romance!

This is the story of one of those pretty creatures who lived on the quicksand of popularity.

Greta Garbo as Marguerite Gautier, the Lady of the Camillias (who is known as Camille)

Robert Taylor as Armand de Valle

Henry Daniel as the Baron

It's 1847, Paris. A very seductive city, from the horse drawn carriages traveling the wide tree-lined boulevards to its wonderful theaters where romance and drama bloom each night in the private boxes high above the main floor.

We first meet Marguerite at the theatre. There is a mix-up of whom she has her opera glasses trained on. Two men, one a Baron, the other is a handsome young man who is smitten with her. He's seen her several times previously and is enchanted by her.

She becomes the Baron's mistress at the same time that she's drawn to the younger man. Juggling the two men in her life comes to an end when the Baron and Armand duel. The Baron is hurt and Armand hides until it all blows over.

Camille is very ill. The Baron has abandoned her. Armand's pride is hurt but he still loves her. He comes to her bedside. We watch a fascinating love scene unfold. Camille is getting out of her sick bed to prepare herself for her lover.

This movie was made when the MGM lion really roared! And yes, they had faces then. After viewing the film, we realize that at all times, everyone had remained fully clothed. We knew that she was a courtesan, but the writers were so adept at writing, the directors so superb at guiding the actors, we knew all that we had to know … that MOVIES ARE MAGIC!

MGM-1936

Black and White

Producer-Irving Thalberg

Director-George Cukor

Art Director-Cedric Gibbons

Costume Design-Adrian

Novel/Play-Alexander Dumas

Cinematography-William H. Daniels

THE HURRICANE

I WORRY ABOUT EVERYTHING WHEN YOU'RE AWAY. ABOUT THE WIND, ABOUT THE WAVES...

Dorothy Lamour as Marama

John Hall as Terangi

Thomas Mitchell as the Island Doctor

A schooner approaches the island of Manakoora in the South Seas. At the top of the mast, a young man is guiding the ship through the dangerous shoals. It's the first mate, Terangi, and he's returning to the island to marry his sweetheart.

Soon the ship is out of danger and they're close to land. He calls out her name as he does a magnificent dive off the top of the mast.

She hears him call out, sees him dive and is soon swimming toward him. Beautiful!

They're married at sundown and a wedding luau is being given in their honor. The Island Doctor is giving a long-winded speech. Marama whispers something into Terangi's ear. They sneak away along the shore where his canoe is waiting. A guitar is playing the haunting song, "The Moon of Manakoora" as he paddles to another part of the island.

Terangi lifts Marama out of the canoe. She puts one of her wedding leis over his shoulders. They kiss. They look at each other longingly. The screen is filled with a beautiful shot of each of their faces. He picks her up and very gently drops to his knees, placing her on the leaves. Next you see the palm moving gently and you swear you smell the blossoms.

Excuse me, I have to call my travel agent!

Samuel Goldwyn-1937

Black and White

Director-John Ford

Novel-Charles Nordhoff and James Hall

Music Score-Alfred Newman

Special Effects-James Basevi

Cinematographer-Bert Glennon

Costume Design-Omar Kiam

GONE WITH THE WIND

Clark Gable as Rhett Butler

Vivian Leigh as Scarlett O'Hara

Olivia DeHavilland as Melanie

Leslie Howard as Ashley

A wonderful supporting cast was assembled. Hattie McDaniel was the first black artist to receive an Academy Award. There's not much that hasn't been said about this film. Every film fan worth his or her salt has to get their *GONE WITH THE WIND* fix at least once a year! It's held up beautifully. Perfect casting. It just "all fits together."

Earlier in the day, two busy-body women catch Scarlett in Ashley's arms. It was really quite innocent, but you know how people talk... and exaggerate. By now, the entire city knows about their foolish indiscretion. She's actually embarrassed and feigns a headache to get out of going to Ashley's birthday party.

Rhett has heard the story by now. He comes into her bedroom, forces her to put on a gown and to get herself ready for the party. He takes her there but doesn't go in, leaving her to her own devices.

Of course, she survives the party. This woman survived the war.

What's a party full of hostile people, particularly when most of them have been your friend at one time or another?

Now, back home in her bedroom, wearing a beautiful red velvet dressing gown, she decides to go downstairs, possibly for a brandy.

We see her descending the majestic stairway.

Rhett calls out, "Come in, Mrs. Butler."

Scarlett enters the drawing room. Rhett has been drinking. They quarrel, she leaves, he follows. He picks her up and starts the long ascent, up that same majestic stairway.

No close-ups, just a wide, long shot of Rhett carrying Scarlett up the stairs. Fade out. What a scene!

Selznick International Pictures/Metro-Goldwyn-Mayer-1939

Technicolor

Director-Victor Fleming

Novel-Margaret Mitchell

Producer-David O. Selznick

Screenplay-Sidney Howard

Music-Max Steiner

Cinematography-Ernest Haller

Costume Design-Walter Plunkett

Production Design-William Cameron Menzies

THE RAINS CAME

IN YOUR HEART MY LOVE HAS FOUND A HOME. AND IT CAN NEVER DIE.

Myrna Loy as Lady Edwina Esketh

Tyrone Power as Major Rama Safti

George Brent as Tom Ransome

With **Brenda Joyce, Nigel Bruce,** and **Maria Ouspenskaya** as The Maharani

India, 1938. The State of Ranchipur. Monsoon weather. Sticky, steamy, exotic! Tom Ransome has two problems. He's a painter with painter's block and he has a drinking problem. He's about to face his third problem. The missionary's daughter has a mad crush on him. He's at their usual Sunday tea party when a messenger from the palace arrives with an invitation from the Maharani. She requests his presence at a dinner party honoring Lord and Lady Esketh.

He puts on his elegant black tail-coat outfit and makes his entrance. The Maharani greets him and takes him to meet the honored guests. Tom is momentarily stunned! He had no idea who they were. LADY EDWINA AND HE WERE ONCE LOVERS!

After dinner, Tom takes Edwina on a tour of the palace. She's bored, world-weary and seems only interested in worldly pleasures. The palace is enormous.

They stop for a rest. He lights her cigarette and through the open windows lightning strikes. Then the rain begins. A breeze billows the curtains. He lights his cigarette. She blows out the match. They're in semi-darkness looking at each other. Obviously, a spark remains… but oh, so subtle.

Outside the rain is hammering the steps, bouncing off the roof, literally filling the streets. Lord Esketh wants to go home. He feels ill from the heat. Where are they?

Tom and Edwina rejoin the party. She spies Major Rama across the room.

Edwina says, "Who is the pale, copper Apollo?"

Tom responds, “Major Rama Safti.”

“Not bad. Not bad at all.”

Tom says, “Don’t waste your time. He’s a surgeon and a scientist. Any interest he might have in romance is purely biological.”

“You make it sound even more exciting,” says Edwina.

Edwina and Major Rama are introduced. And so, starts Lady Edwina’s seduction of Major Rama.

The next day, she calls him to look in on her husband. The following day she invites him to ride. It begins to pour. They find shelter in the Maharani’s music conservatory. They enter one of the rooms. A famous Indian singer is performing with his musicians.

Rama repeats the words to her in English as the singer says them, “It’s a love song. The words are tender, promising undying love.”

She can’t take her eyes off him. She is making a fatal mistake, allowing herself to fall in love. She is being seduced not only by his beauty but by his goodness.

This film has wonderful special effects of earthquakes and monsoons all by Fred Sersen.

20th Century Fox 1939

Black and White

Producer-Daryl F. Zanuck

Director-Clarence Leon Brown

Novel-Louis Bromfield

Cinematographer-Arthur Miller

Costume Design-Gwen Wakeling

BLOOD AND SAND

IF THIS IS DEATH IN THE AFTERNOON, THEN SHE'S DEATH IN THE EVENING. (Laird Cregar says this about Dona Sol, played by Rita Hayworth, in reference to the bullfight they are attending.)

Rita Hayworth as Dona Sol

Tyrone Power as Juan Gallardo

Linda Darnell as Carmen Espinosa

This seduction begins the moment their eyes meet.

Tyrone has just finished putting on his matador suit. All the well-wishers and hangers-on have gone. He slips into the chapel to pray. Rita is showing her present lover the sites. Tyrone finishes praying, turns to leave and their eyes not only meet, but they also lock! He walks past her, but you know this is just the beginning.

Now he's inside the bullring, walking around the perimeter greeting the audience. He looks up and there she is. Their eyes meet again. Strike two!

He warms up with some fancy cape work. Rita throws him a single red rose. How often do you see that in a movie, a woman throwing a man a rose?

He dedicates the bull to her and throws her his montera (hat)! He kills the bull, and she throws him a bouquet of red roses! Strike Three! He's out!

The next morning, a note arrives from Rita. If you want your hat, come to my casa and get it. Then she shares the address. Three million guys wrote down that address and went there AND no Rita. Just an empty lot!

The very next scene, Tyrone is Rita's guest at a magnificent dinner party. They've dined and the guests are leaving to go to a concert. Rita begs off via a headache, her French lover senses that this matador will be her new conquest. They part amicably. He even gives her a ring as a token of his friendship. All very civilized.

Now the two are alone on the veranda. She plays the guitar and sings for him. He falls asleep. She's mad, then laughs and goes off to bed.

The bells chime at three a.m., he wakes up embarrassed and walks down the hall, trying all the doors until he finds her bedroom. Now she's sleeping. He stares at her. The camera moves closer. He's stunned by her beauty.

The next morning, he brings his wife a beautiful necklace, a little guilty conscience. He kisses her and we now see that ring on his finger. Now, that's subtle seduction! (Beautiful Linda Darnell is the wife. She believes he was really out with the boys.)

So, the next time your husband gives you a gift for no reason at all, you've every right to be suspicious! Take the gift, then argue. Check the newspapers and see what bullring he's fighting in. ¡Ole, Rita, Tyrone, and Linda! ¡Ole!

20th Century Fox-1941

Director-Rouben Mamoulian

Producer-Daryl Zanuck

Writers-Jo Swerling, Vicente Blasco Ibanez

Cinematography-Ernest Palmer, Ray Rennahan

Costume Design-Travis Banton

NOW VOYAGER

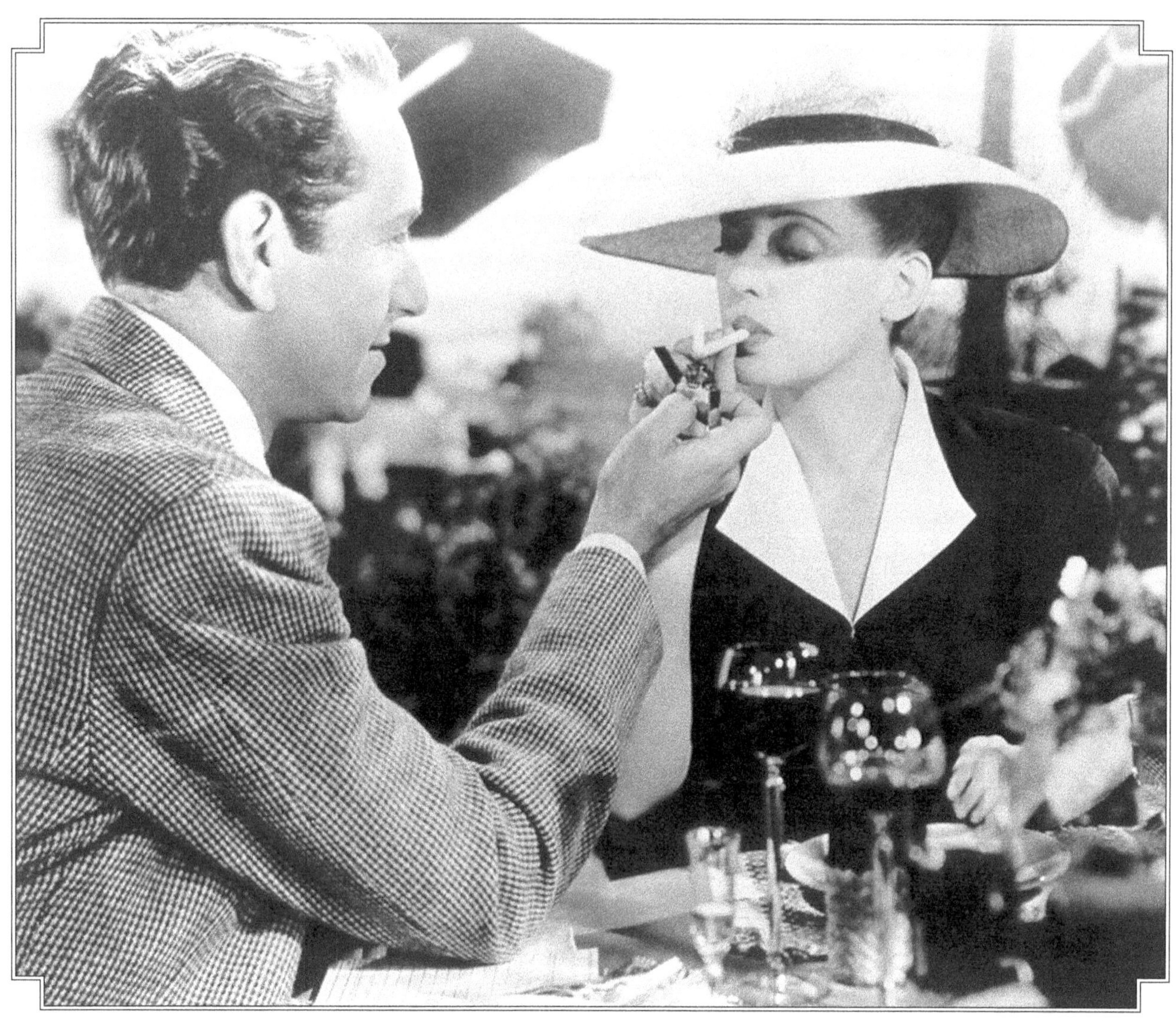

JERRY, LET'S DON'T ASK FOR THE MOON. WE HAVE THE STARS.

Bette Davis as Charlotte Vale

Paul Henreid as Jerry

Claude Rains as Dr. Jackworth

This is one of the most romantic films ever made! It takes Bette Davis from an ugly duckling to a magnificent swan with a glamorous wardrobe by her favorite designer, Orry-Kelly.

Paul Henreid is perfect as Jerry. Very continental. And great at lighting two cigarettes at a time. This became a very popular practice, emulated by many who ended up with burnt fingers or scorched noses! We'll do anything to look suave like movie stars.

They meet on a cruise. She's recovering from a nervous breakdown brought on by her cold, domineering mother. The psychiatrist was Claude Raines-warm, caring and firm. They become, over the months, great friends. He recommends this cruise. What a smart man!

When she boards the ship, gone is the unattractive, insecure person. Instead, we see a stunning woman in a large hat. What a revelation!

Jerry sees her and is immediately attracted to her. She is chic, aloof but terribly frightened. He's charming and admits that he's married unhappily. Their romance blooms. They spend days in various ports and nights on the ship, dining and getting acquainted.

In Rio de Janeiro, Jerry hires a tour guide who gets lost in the mountains, backs the car over a small hill and leaves to get help. This leaves our lovers in a mountain cabin. They build a roaring fire. She falls asleep. He kisses her softly so as not to wake her.

The next scene is beautiful.

He climbs over his balcony to hers. They discuss life-love-happiness.

Charlotte says, "Mercy, no. I'm immune to happiness."

Jerry responds, "If I were free, there would be only one thing I would do. Prove that you're not immune to happiness. My darling, you're crying."

"I'm such a fool, such an old fool. These are only tears of

gratitude, an old maid's gratitude. You see, no one's ever called me darling before."

They kiss!

Charlotte says, "Let me go."

They kiss again. All the while, the theme song is playing.

Would it be wrong to stay? Ah, those Bette Davis eyes!

Warner Brothers-1942

Producer-Hal Wallis

Music-Max Steiner

Cinematography-Sol Polito

Costume Design-Orry-Kelly

CASABLANCA

OF ALL THE GIN JOINTS IN ALL THE TOWNS IN ALL THE WORLD, SHE WALKS INTO MINE.

Humphrey Bogart as Rick (Richard) Blaine

Ingrid Bergman as Ilsa

Paul Henreid as her husband, Victor Laszlo

Claude Raines as Renault, the Vichy Police Captain

Dooley Wilson as Sam

Has there ever been a more perfectly cast movie? From the stars, the supporting actors, to the bit players, it was truly magic! If this movie is not in your collection, it is not too late to make amends.

Over the years, we've all heard an assortment of stories about the making of *CASABLANCA*. All the tales, including which actor was, or was not, being considered including new pages arriving on the set each morning to be shot that day, have all helped create the wonderful aura around this film.

Here is the seduction scene-very subtle. (The powerful Breen Office oversaw our country's morals on the silver screen at that time. The Breen office was the censorship office of the Golden Age of Hollywood.)

Rick's Café Américain has been closed by Major Strasser. Victor has snuck out to an underground meeting. Ilsa goes to Rick, begging for the exit visas, pleading that he is the last hope, etc. They quarrel. She walks away then turns around. There's a gun in her hand.

Rick says, "Go ahead and shoot. You'll be doing me a favor."

"Richard, I tried to stay away. I thought I would never see you again, that you were out of my life."

She begins to cry. He goes to her.

She says, "The day you left Paris. If you know what I went through. If you knew how much I loved you. How much I still love you."

They kiss. And all the while "As Time Goes By" is playing in the background.

The next shot is of the beacon shining and turning through the night haze.

Take that! The supporting cast is only wonderful! Peter Lorre, Sidney Greenstreet, Conrad Veidt as Major Strasser and S.C. Zackel as Max, the headwaiter at Rick's. Wonderful Sets! Great atmosphere!

Warner Brothers-1943

Black and White

Director-Michael Curtiz

Producer-Hal Wallis

Art Director-Carl Jules Weyl

Score-Max Steiner

Cinematographer-Arthur Edeson

Costume Design-Orry-Kelly

"As Time Goes By"-Herman Hapfeld

From an unproduced play entitled *Everybody Comes to Rick's*-M. Burnett and J. Allison

CASABLANCA

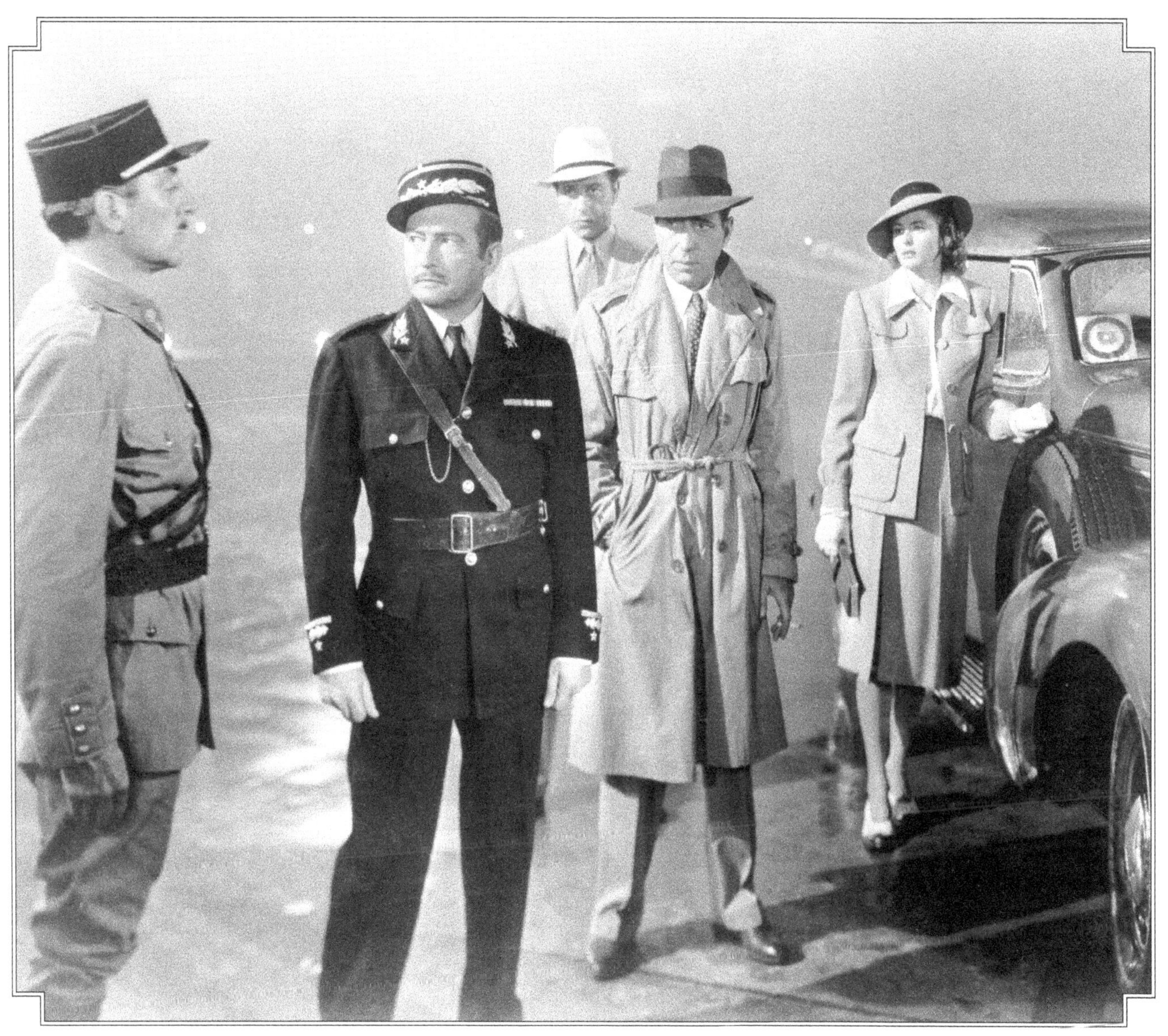

FOR WHOM THE BELL TOLLS

Ingrid Bergman as Maria

Gary Cooper as Robert Jordan

The Spanish Civil War was the backdrop for this film version of Ernest Hemmingway's novel, *For Whom the Bell Tolls.*

Ingrid Bergman and Gary Cooper were the lovers. You have never seen so many close-ups of two beautiful people in one film! She plays Maria, a fighter for the Republic. He plays Robert, an American mercenary, sent to help these fighters blow up a bridge.

> When he arrives, she's bringing food to the fighters. Their eyes meet and we know they're destined to be more than just a man and a woman fighting on the same side. They talk and he tells her he has no time for anything but the way. And, of course, we believe him, for at least two seconds.
>
> She looks like a million bucks-in cash. She's wearing a man's shirt and pants and has hair as short as his, which embarrasses her. She keeps running her hands through it. He keeps running his hands through it.

Every man in the audience wants to run his hands through it!

> Gary is about to drop off to sleep. He hears noises. It's Ingrid coming to warn him about Pablo, one of the fighters she doesn't trust. They hear the sound of someone approaching. It's Pablo. Gary pulls her under the blanket. Pablo walks by.
>
> She pulls the blanket off her head, and he runs his fingers through her hair to smooth it out.
>
> Robert says, "Did I muss you?"
>
> Maria answers, "All day I wanted you to do that."
>
> Robert says, "Me, too" and she looks at him, smiles-fades out.

Every male in the audience felt a little something in the pit of his stomach and every female ran out to buy some scissors in case he showed up.

The next shot shows Gary waking up in the morning alone. Now, that's romantic!

Paramount Pictures-1943

Technicolor

Director-Sam Wood

Cinematography-Ray Rennahan

Production Design-William Cameron Menzies

Costume Design-Edith Head

MURDER, MY SWEET

VELMA, SHE WAS CUTE AS LACE PANTS-A REDHEAD.

Dick Powell as Phillip Marlowe

Claire Trevor as Helen/Mrs. Grayle

Mike Mazurke as Joe "Moose" Malloy

Anne Shirley as Ann Grayle

Otto Kruger as Jules Amthor

Los Angeles in the 1940s. Philip Marlowe is hired by Moose Malloy to find his girlfriend. He'd been sent away for eight years. She quit writing to him six years ago. Velma was her name. Moose insists on taking Marlowe to the seedy club where Velma used to work.

From then on, it's a real roller-coaster ride. No one is who you think they are OR who they say they are. It's full of twists and turns, charlatans, fancy apartments, bad doctors with syringes full of dope, wonderful beach houses, and a missing jade necklace.

This time the black widow spider comes in the form of a gorgeous blonde. At their first meeting, Mrs. Grayle is sitting in a big chair, her skirt is hiked up above her knees to show her sun-tanned legs. A white two-piece, short-sleeved outfit with a bare midriff. Four or five gardenias are nesting in her blonde hair. What a piece of work!

She goes to work on him immediately, nestling back in her chair, little by little moving closer to him. She's done this before.

The next time they meet, she comes to his apartment in a beautiful black, sparkly gown-reminds you of a shiny black spider! And the woman is spinning a web of lies, intrigue, shamelessness and believes in every word that she says.

Each time Marlowe and Mrs. Grayle meet, she seduces him a little more-her perfume, big eyes, husky voice, the gardenias

```
in her hair and the promise of a lot of money. We all know guys
who gave in to just one of these temptations, but Philip Marlowe
is not easy.
```

What a fascinating film-a great film noir!

This film was released under two titles, *MURDER, MY SWEET* and *FAREWELL, MY LOVELY*.

RKO-1944

Black and White

Director-Edward Dmytryk

Novel-*Farewell, My Lovely* by Raymond Chandler

Costume Design-Edward Stevenson

Cinematography-Harry J. Wild

Art Direction-Carroll Clark, Albert S. D'Agostino

TO HAVE AND HAVE NOT

I'M HARD TO GET, STEVE. ALL YOU HAVE TO DO IS ASK ME.

Humphrey Bogart as Harry "Steve" Morgan

Walter Brennan as Eddie

Hoagy Carmichael as Cricket, the piano player at "Frenchies"

And introducing a New Screen Sensation: Lauren Bacall as Marie whom Bogart nicknamed "Slim"

Humphrey Bogart sheds that impeccable white dinner jacket and trench coat from *CASABLANCA* to don the clothes (and hat) as the skipper of a small charter boat on the French island of Martinique.

> It's 1940. The French and the Germans are at war. Most of the activity takes place in "Frenchies." It's a nightclub with rooms upstairs full of assorted characters and a basement hiding the Free French: waiting to make their escape. Busy! No wonder the French Police watched "Frenchies" night and day.
>
> At their first meeting, Harry is in his room, the door is open. A voice behind him asks "Anybody got a match?" He turns to see who it is. She's leaning against the door. He throws her the matches, she catches them, lights her cigarette and says "Thanks," then throws the matches back to him. No names exchanged but she definitely has his attention.

Much of the film is spent going back and forth to each other's rooms, quarreling, teasing, needling each other and Bogart's attempt to establish boundaries. Bacall is trying to get inside his boundaries.

It's great fun! The dialogue is crisp. They finally kiss... She's leaving and says these wonderful lines-full of innuendo, "You know how to whistle, don't you, Steve? You just put your lips together and blow."

Later on, she almost gets him into the bathtub. And he'll shave! But they're interrupted. And still, no overt sex. How did they do it? Maybe taste, style, good scripts, and a lot of self-respect and respect for each other. Could you imagine Humphrey Bogart allowing anyone to see anything that wasn't necessary between himself and his leading ladies? Not on your life. He became everyone's favorite version of the tough guy-masculine, cynical, trustworthy. If anyone could get us out of a scrape, he could.

Lauren Bacall was truly one of a kind. No one had her special style, delivery, screen persona. They named her "The Look."

Walter Brennan was a character actor right from the beginning and gave every role he played something special. He was a sidekick to almost every major actor-sometimes comic, sometimes a little pathetic alcoholic, but he always commanded your attention.

Hoagy Carmichael was a prolific song writer and enjoyed a good career in film. He co-wrote two of the three songs that he sang and played in the film. Johnny Mercer wrote the lyrics for "How Little We Know" which Lauren Bacall sang. Stanley Adams wrote the lyrics to "Hong Kong Blues."

The cast was great. Marcel Dalio, the beautiful Dolores Moran, and Dan Seymour as the insidious Captain Renard.

Warner Brothers-1944

Black and White

Director-Howard Hawks

Novel-Ernest Hemingway

Screenplay-William Faulkner, Jules Furthman

Cinematographer-Sid Hickox

Costume Design-Milo Anderson

Art Director-Charles Novi

Music-Franz Waxman

DOUBLE INDEMNITY

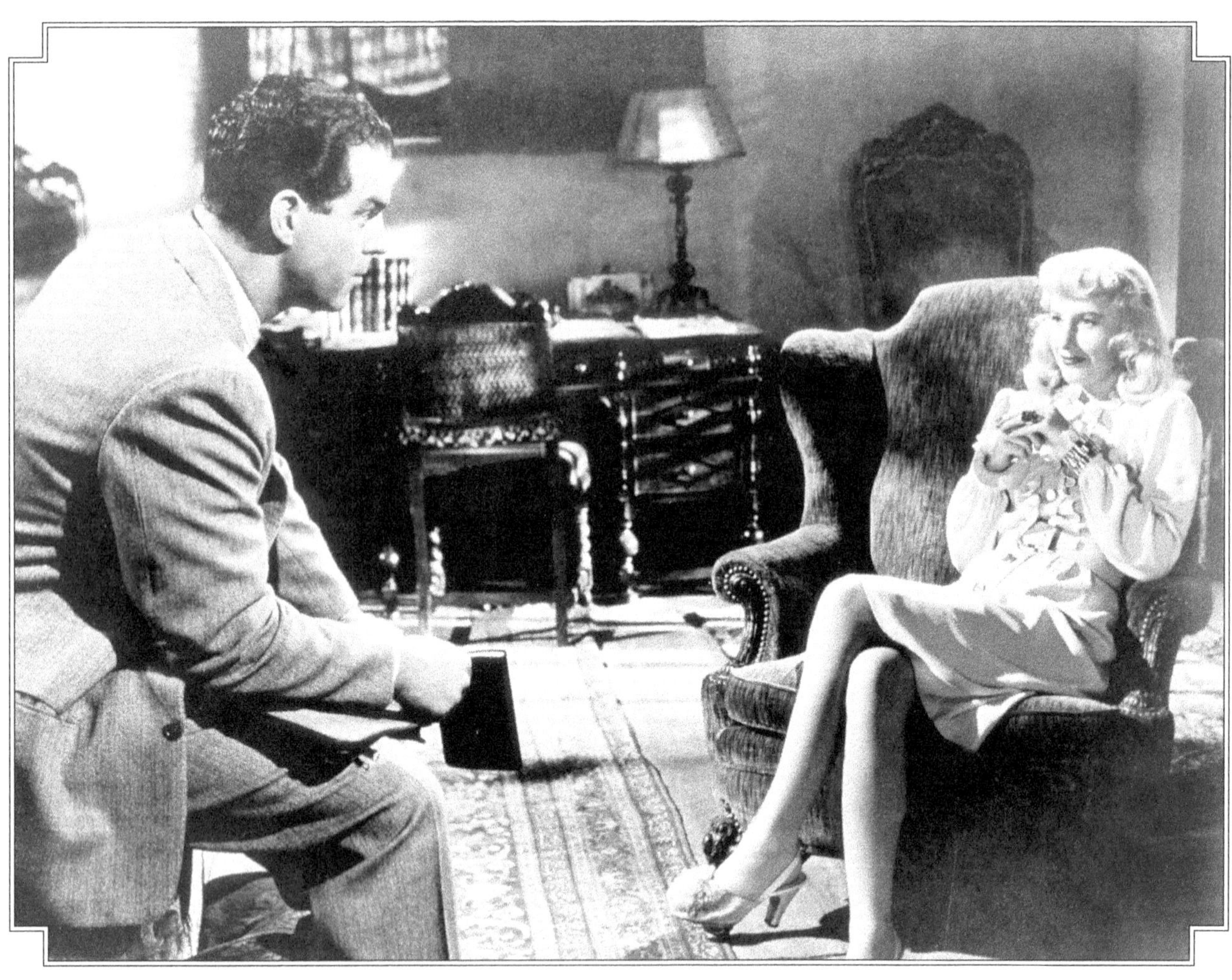

THAT'S A HONEY OF AN ANKLET YOU'RE WEARING, MRS. DIETRICHSON.

Fred MacMurray as Neff

Barbara Stanwyck as the wife, Phyllis

Edward G. Robinson as Keys

Fred MacMurray is Neff, an insurance salesman going to renew an auto policy. He finds the man of the house is out, but his wife is certainly in. Standing at the top of the stairs, almost wrapped in a towel, Barbara Stanwyck is the wife, Phyllis.

She asks him to wait while she puts something on. He will and he does. The camera stays on her legs the entire walk down the steps, an ankle bracelet sending out its own gleaming message.

He gets the message.

They discuss the insurance policy sparing back and forth - innuendos flying, (tart dialogue from the director, Billy Wilder and Raymond Chandler from a James M. Cain story). She tries playing it straight, but he reads her like a book. They make an appointment to discuss the policy with her husband. She calls and makes the appointment for another day, late in the afternoon.

They meet. More shots of her great legs and the ankle bracelet. They discuss a double indemnity insurance policy-accidental death. They quarrel. He leaves.

But he cannot get her out of his insides. His doorbell rings and it's her. Many hugs and kisses later, they agree on a plan. She leaves.

They commit the crime, but the insurance investigator, Keyes, won't pay the claim that easy. It's too perfect. He becomes obsessed with the case; he thinks it was murder.

His doorbell rings and it's Keyes, wanting to discuss the case looking for flaws. While they're talking, she comes up to the door and hears the conversation and hides. Keyes leaves. She comes into the apartment and all the tension spills out.

Neff says, "Afraid, baby?"

"Yes, I'm afraid, but not of Keyes. I'm afraid of us. We're not the same anymore. We did this so we could be together, but instead it's pulling us apart. Isn't it Walter?"

"What are you talking about?"

Phyllis says, "And you don't really care if we see each other or not?"

Neff answers, "Shut up, baby." And he pulls her to him.

This entire scene is played in suits-the usual for men. Barbara is in black pinstripes, courtesy of Edith Head.

Paramount Pictures-1944

Black and White

Director-Billy Wilder

Novel-James M. Cain

Costume Design-Edith Head

DOUBLE INDEMNITY

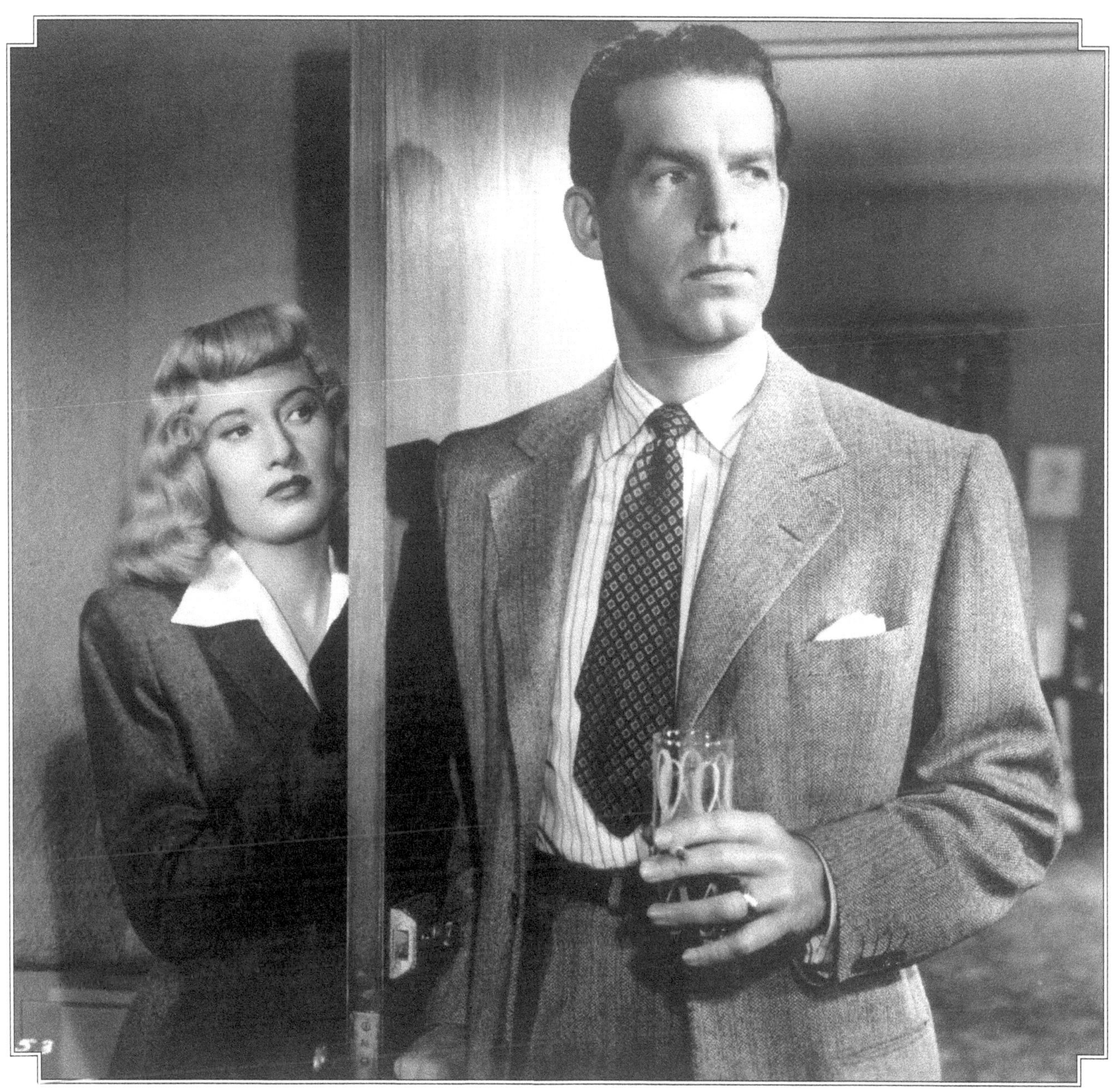

THE PORTRAIT OF DORIAN GRAY

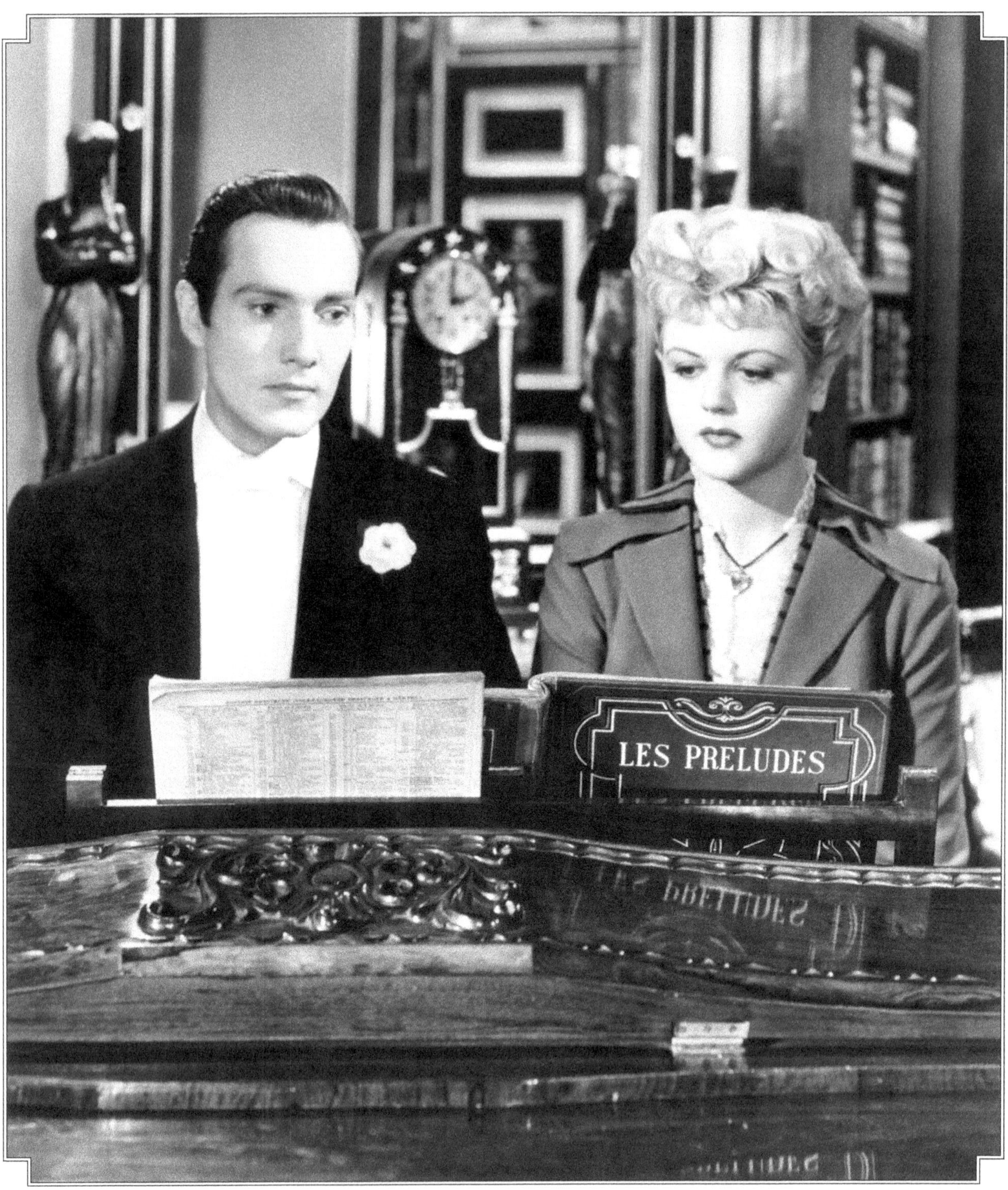

AS I GROW OLD, THIS PICTURE WILL ALWAYS BE YOUNG.

Hurd Hatfield as Dorian Gray

Angela Lansbury as Sibyl Vane

George Saunders as Lord Henry Wooten

"Live, let nothing be lost upon you." The words of cynical Lord Henry ring in Dorian's ears. So begins his quest. This journey takes him from Mayfair to the seamier parts of London.

> He enters the pub "The Two Turtles." He sits, waiting for something to happen.
>
> The curtains part on a small stage. A lovely young woman is standing here, in tableau, fake snow falling around her. She begins to sing "Good-bye, Little Yellow Bird" and wanders down into the audience.
>
> THEIR EYES MEET-NOT A WORD IS SPOKEN YET WE KNOW THIS IS THEIR BEGINNING! Night after night, he returns to the pub to hear her sing. AND still no words are spoken. One night after the show, he goes backstage and asks her to sing, just for him. This is how their courtship begins.
>
> He wants to marry her, though Lord Henry suggests that before marriage, Dorian should test Sibyl to see if she is good enough for him. Dorian follows his advice, inviting her to his home to see the recently finished portrait of himself.
>
> They've spent the evening together and Sibyl prepares to leave. Dorian is seated at the piano. He asks her not to go. She is stunned! Yet, she loves him very much. But it's terribly improper in Victorian England. She goes towards the door, changes her mind. And we see her standing by the piano.

Not a word was spoken!

Metro-Goldyn-Mayer-1945

Black and White (the exception being the portrait which is always shown in color)

Director-Albert Lewin

Novel-Oscar Wilde

Art Direction-Cedric Gibbons

Cinematography-Harry Stradling, Sr. was Oscar nominated, as was Angela Lansbury!

Costume Design-Valles

GILDA

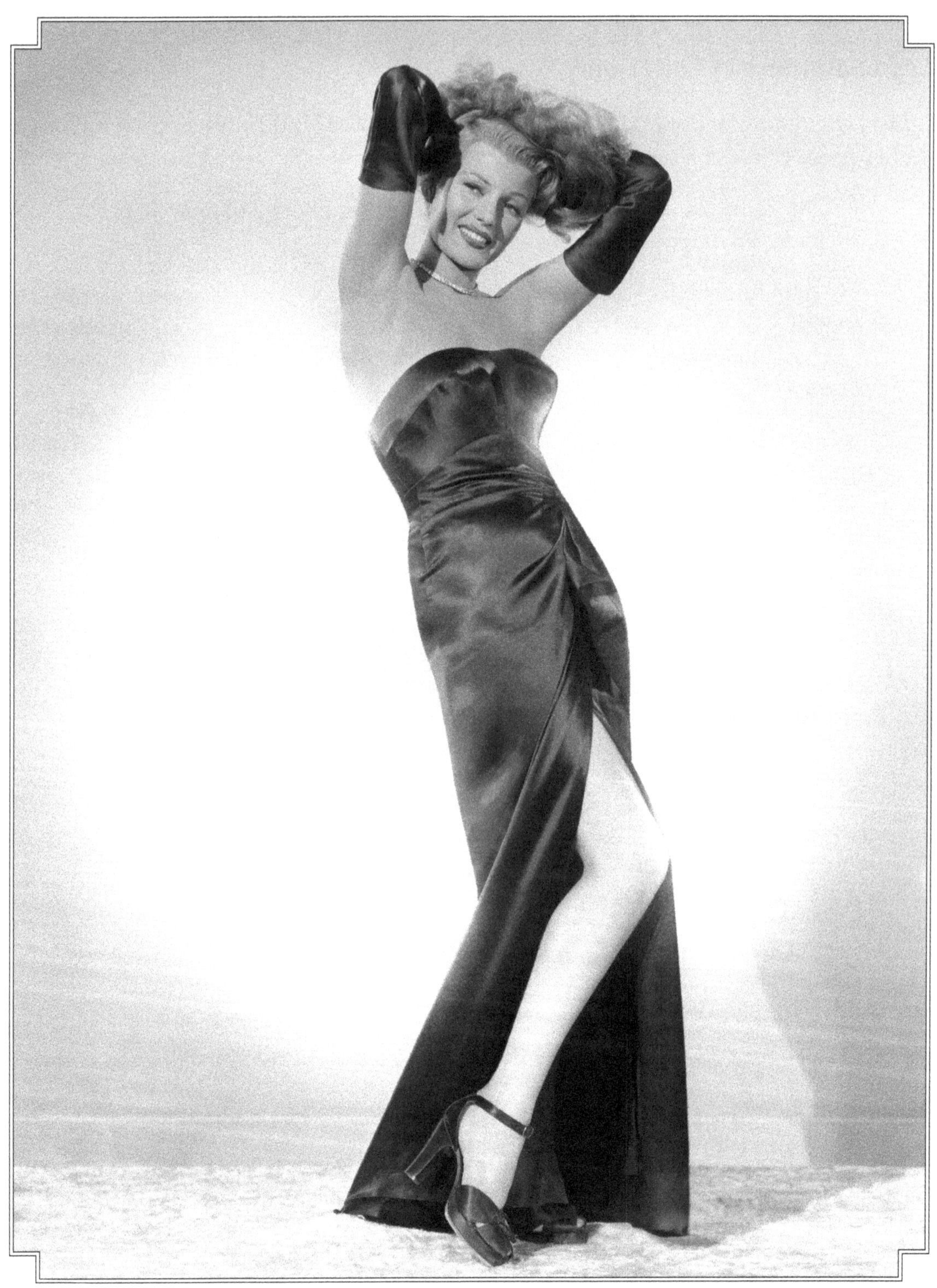

HATE CAN BE A VERY EXCITING EMOTION. HAVE YOU NOTICED THAT?

Rita Hayworth as Gilda (a woman with a questionable past)

Glenn Ford as Johnny Farrell

George Macready as Ballin Mundson

Ballin Mundson, as played by George Macready, is a more wonderfully sinister villain than you've ever met. Gilda marries Mundson on the rebound from Johnny. What a trio! And this film moves! What sets! What costumes! What photography!

This movie sealed Rita's fate. She was known henceforth as The Love Goddess. From the moment she throws back her head and that gorgeous mane of hair whirls around, her sensational face fills the screen, and we are mesmerized. Such grace and beauty. The lady seduced an entire film audience.

But the part of the film that clinched it was her "Put the Blame on Mame" song and dance number. Taking off only her elbow length black gloves and a thin silver necklace, she danced the entire number in a full-length black dress slit up to the thigh.

Yes, folks, she seduced all of us and she did it with her clothes on! It's called talent.

Columbia Pictures-1946

Black and White

Director-Charles Vidor

Cinematographer-Rudolph Maté

Costume Design-Jean Louis

DUEL IN THE SUN

FOR WHEN THE SUN IS LOW AND THE COLD WIND BLOWS ACROSS THE DESERT, THERE ARE THOSE OF INDIAN BLOOD WHO STILL SPEAK OF PEARL CHAVEZ, THE HALF-BREED GIRL FROM DOWN ALONG THE BORDER AND THE LAUGHING OUTLAW WITH WHOM SHE KEPT A FINAL RENDEZVOUS.

Jennifer Jones as Pearl

Gregory Peck as Luton

Joseph Cotton as Jesse

Butterfly McQueen as Vashti

This movie was supposed to do for Texas what *GONE WITH THE WIND* did for the South. It didn't, but it's still great fun. It has the U.S. Cavalry, Chinese coolies building a railroad, and Butterfly McQueen as Vashti, the maid, stealing every scene she's in. Plus, a most unusual ending-a shootout between Pearl and Luton, all in glorious burning color.

A lone figure of a man on a horse is approaching the ranch. The sky looks angry-black and grey-wind blowing-lightening flashing. It's late. Trying to beat the storm, he gallops up to the barn, puts his horse away and notices no one is around except Vashti, singing to herself.

He asks where everyone is. This conversation sends him out for a smoke on the veranda.

Hearing noises from Pearl's room, a sly grin appears on his face, and he meanders that-a-way.

We see Pearl on her hands and knees scrubbing the floor. He steps into the room. She can feel that someone is there. Turning, she looks at him. He closes the door. He takes off his hat, planning to stay awhile. She hurls the scrub rag in his face. He grabs and kisses her then lets her go. She then grabs him and doesn't let go. Through the window, we see lightning, we hear thunder and wind.

And I'm not kidding! These two were so beautiful together.

Jennifer-with those off-the-shoulder peasant blouses, flowing skirts, and big yellow flowers in her hair. Gregory-tall, lanky, insolent.

I wonder when the next buckboard leaves for the ranch!

Selznick International-1946

Director-King Vidor

Script-David O. Selznick

Production Design-J. McMillan Johnson

Costume Design-Walter Plunkett

HUMOREQUE

YOU MIGHT BE SORRY LOVE WAS EVER INVENTED, PAUL.

Joan Crawford as Helen Wright

John Garfield as Paul Boray

Oscar Levant as Sid Jeffries

John Garfield is Paul Boray, a young, struggling violinist who's come up the hard way, rough around the edges and with a chip on his shoulder. His friend and pianist/conductor, Sid, is playing at a posh party and takes Paul along. A pretty girl doesn't believe that he's a violinist and needles him into playing. Sid accompanies him.

Helen Wright is the hostess. She hears him playing, puts on her glasses to see who it is… and we're off! She has an edge to her, drinks too much, and is very bored. And she loves the company of young, good-looking men around her.

The next day, a gift arrives for him… a gold cigarette case. She's making peace. She becomes his mentor, introduces him to the right people, and his career takes off. Still, there's a strange undertone in their relationship.

Here's the scene that starts their affair.

They go to her beach home, swim, have lunch, and go horseback riding. She's ahead of him, looks back to see where he is, and a low-hanging branch knocks her off her horse. She's dazed. He rushes to her side.

Helen says, "I'm alright. Leave me alone!"

"But your shirt's torn." He kisses her.

"Leave me alone, Paul."

WAVES BREAK… a beautiful shot of the ocean. Night falls. So did Joan and so did John!

Joan looks magnificent in this film!

Warner Brothers-1946

Black and White

Director-John Negulesco

Script-Clifford Odets from a Fanny Hurst novel

Costume Design-Adrian

Cinematographer-Ernest Haller

Music Director-Franz Waxman

Violin played-Isaac Stern

THE POSTMAN ALWAYS RINGS TWICE

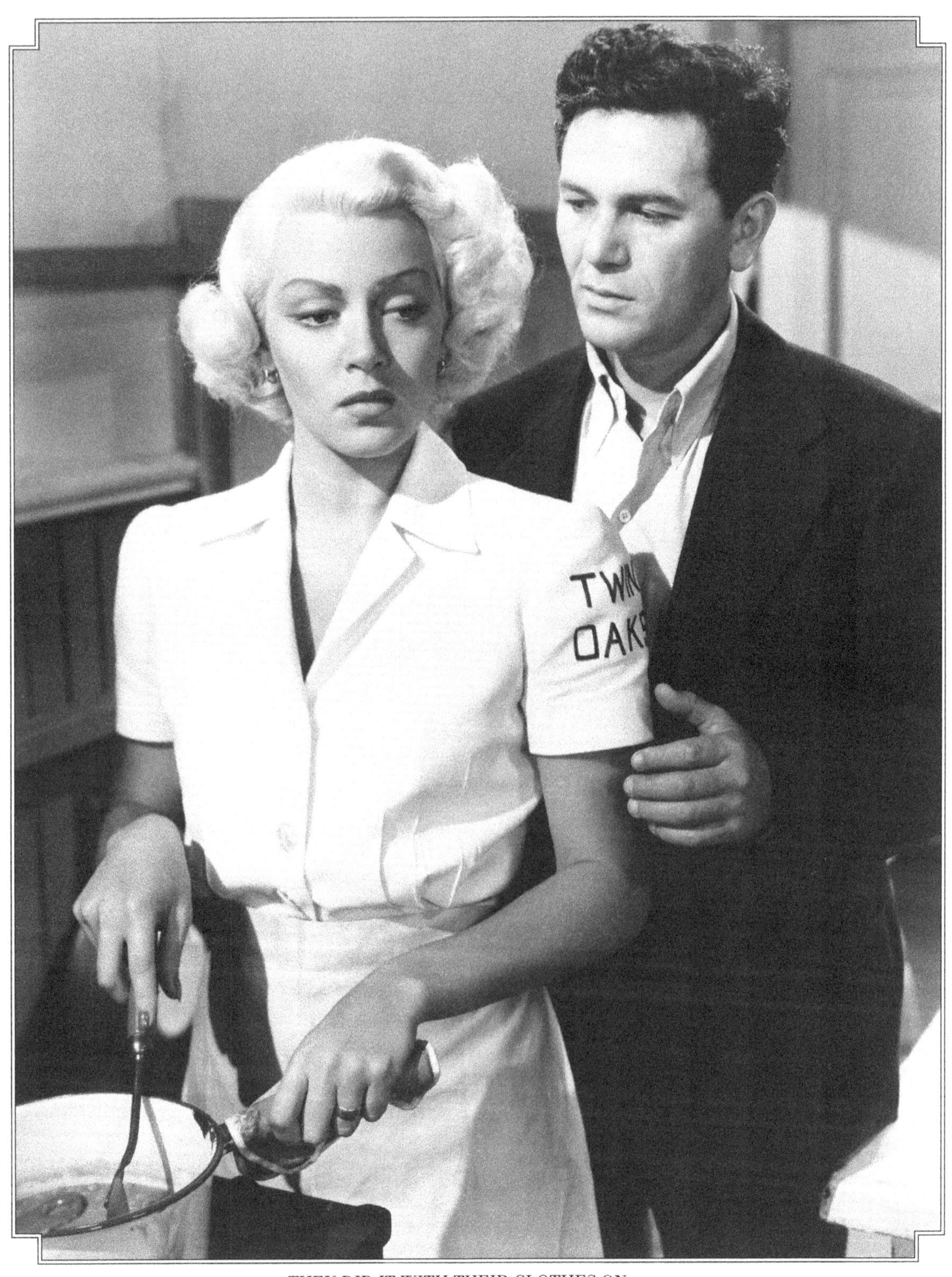

'CAUSE WE'RE CHAINED TO EACH OTHER, CORA.

Lana Turner as Cora Smith

John Garfield as Frank Chambers

Lana Turner oozes sex. She was five feet three inches tall and made of blonde dynamite.

This movie is based on the James M. Cain novel. The book was considered not filmable. However, the screen writers managed to turn out a script that squeaked past the censors while still retaining much of the heat of the book.

Frank Chambers is a drifter who happens along the wayside restaurant that Lana's husband owns. He makes the mistake of hiring Frank as a combination gas station attendant and handyman AND he certainly was!

Filmed in black and white, the film did not need color. Lana's hair was so platinum, it glowed. She's in dazzling white almost the entire time.

From the moment we see her lipstick roll across the floor and see John turn to her, we see that she's standing there in white shorts, top and turban and then a close-up of that face. It was all over. He was hooked and every male in the audience who was over eleven years old had a dry throat.

> Cora's in the kitchen scraping food off the plates. Frank walks in. He's already locked the front door and he makes his move. You can hear what he's thinking. You hear the door rattle. Cora asks if it's locked. He says, "Yes, I locked it." She murmurs that whoever it was went away.
>
> And then they kiss and kiss... the background music swells... the song playing is "She's Funny That Way."

Now, that's seduction!

Metro-Goldwyn-Mayer-1946

Black and White

Director-Tay Garnett

Novel-James M. Cain

Cinematographer-Sidney Wagner

Costume Design-Irene

THE POSTMAN ALWAYS RINGS TWICE

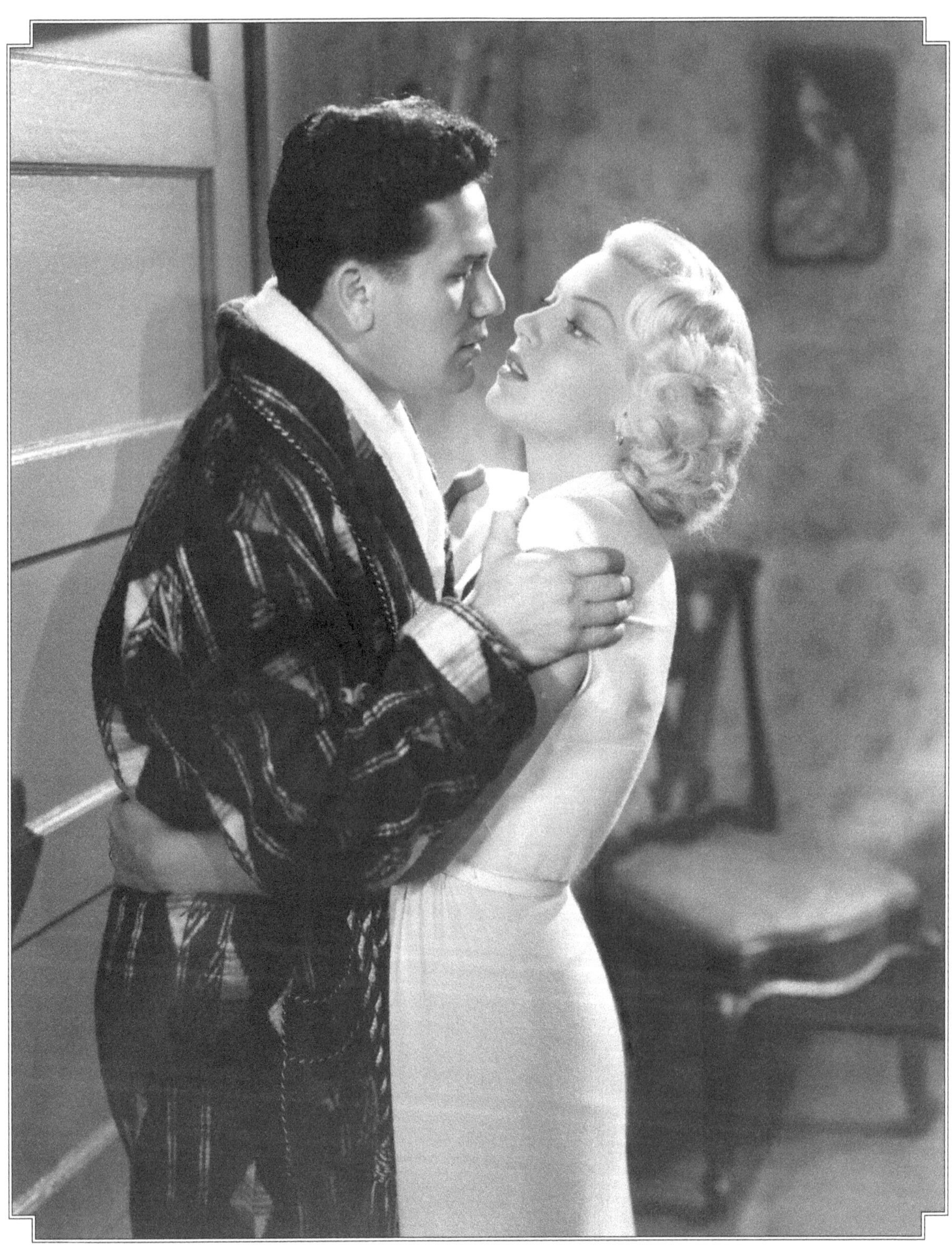

THE KILLERS

I'M POISON, SWEDE-TO MYSELF AND EVERYONE ELSE AROUND ME.

Ava Gardner as Kitty Collins

Burt Lancaster as Swede

Edmond O'Brien as Reardon, the smart insurance man who puts it all together!

Swede is a boxer who just fought and lost his last fight. His hands are shot-too many broken bones. He must find another line of work.

He goes to a fancy party to meet "some people." This is the first time he sees Kitty. She's sitting on the piano bench with the pianist humming a song. We see her back first, gorgeous black hair spilling down her back wearing a black evening gown with a lot of bare shoulder. Swede wants to meet her. When they come face to face, he's stunned! What a beautiful woman! Green eyes, big cleft in her chin, sultry. He blatantly ignores his date. Kitty barely acknowledges him… for now.

Swede becomes involved with her gangster boyfriend. They rob a hat factory. She comes to his room at two o'clock in the morning to warn him of their plan to cut him out of his share of the take. Of course, it's all part of the plot, which has many surprises.

Kitty is totally amoral, dangerous, with not a single principle. She tells lies, lies, lies.

Kitty knocks on the door, comes in, and starts spilling her guts. She takes off her coat... I wonder what she has in mind.

Kitty says, "You won't give me away. You know why Colfax hates you.. because of me. He's no fool. He sees what happened."

Swede replies, "You're not meeting him tomorrow!"

"Alright, Swede." KISS

And she spins her deceitful web. Short, vibrant, enough. AND you know she's ruining him.

MGM lent Ava to Universal. This picture did well. When she returned to MGM, it was with more important roles in major films. She was on her way! It didn't hurt Burt's career, either. Paramount did several major films with him. These two stars were reunited in *SEVEN DAYS IN MAY* in 1964.

Universal-1946

Black and White

Director-Robert Siodmak

Story-Ernest Hemingway

Producer-Mark Hellinger

OUT OF THE PAST

YOU'RE LIKE A LEAF THAT BLOWS FROM ONE GUTTER TO THE NEXT.

Robert Mitchum as Jeff

Jane Greer as Kathie

Kirk Douglas as Whit

This is Robert Mitchum's first starring role, cynical with bedroom eyes. Jane Greer, unblinkingly cold one minute, sweet and loving the next, telling everyone wonderful lies.

Robert is hired by Kirk to find Jane after attempting to kill him and runs away with $40,000. He tails her to Acapulco and looks and waits. She finally appears in a cantina, aloof with big eyes. You know she couldn't have done what Kirk said, not our Jane. They have a drink. She tells him of another bar she frequents that plays American music. He takes the hook, goes to the bar and two nights later, she appears.

SHE WALKED IN AND OUT OF THE MOONLIGHT-SMILING.

They drink, then go to a gambling casino. He's restless.

Kathie says, "Tell me why you're so hard to please."

Jeff says, "Take me where I can tell you."

They walk on the beach. Oh, the moonlight, the breeze in her hair, the waves pounding on the shore. They kiss with a long shot of the ocean-shimmering, dangerous. And you know he is never going to take her back to Kirk.

Great film noir.

RKO-1947

Black and White

Director-Jacques Tourneur

Screenplay-Daniel Mainwaring/Geoffrey Homes

Cinematography-Nicholas Musuraca

Costume Design-Edward Stevenson

GOLDEN EARRINGS

SO, TONIGHT, WHEN THE SPIRITS COME OUT OF THE RIVER, I WILL THANK THEM FOR YOU.

Marlene Dietrich as Lydia, the Gypsy Woman

Ray Milland as the very British Colonel Ralph Denniston

It's 1946, just after the war. In London, at a stuffy men's club, a small package arrives for the now retired Colonel. He opens it and is ecstatic! It's the pair of gold earrings that he left with Lydia, his Gypsy love.

He catches the next available plane to Paris. Sitting next to him is an American who keeps staring at his pierced ears. He senses the man wants to ask why they are pierced.

He shares his story.

Just prior to World War II, he is in Germany on a hush-hush mission. Running from the Nazis, he hides in the hills. He comes upon a campfire, smells food cooking, and sees a figure huddled over the fire. It's Lydia, the Gypsy. She invites him to eat and, before you can say Marlene Dietrich, he's traveling with her in a horse-drawn wagon. So begins their adventure.

Soon she considers him "her man." He fights it, but what can you do when a Gypsy puts a spell on you! And he needs her help to find the sympathetic German doctor who has the formula for the poisonous gas.

Then, he asks her to make him into a Gypsy. She heats up some stain, gives him her late husband's clothes, pierces his ears, and puts in the golden earrings. Now, he's really her man. The violins begin to play. He is now a "Gypsy."

They find the doctor, get the formula, and escape the Nazis. She guides him to the river where he can escape. It's early morning. They're exhausted. They sit down. She caresses his face.

Lydia says, "Oh, Liebling-you lay a spell on me. My head go round and round. I feel weak and frightened. To me, nothing matters, only you. All my life, I believe if I do not love one man, I love another. But now it's different. It's like having a sickness."

The Colonel responds, "No, you never knew what love was. And I never knew what life was. Now we become like each other, merged into each other."

Kiss. Kiss.

Marlene is really something to see, a chain of coins dangling from her long, dark hair. Many layers of blouses and scarves, peasant skirts, and dusky skin. I'd like to see more of her gorgeous gams but... Anyway, a fun picture. Pure 1940s.

Paramount-1947

Black and White

Director-Mitchell Leisen

Cinematography-Daniel L. Fapp

Costume Design-Mary Kay Dodson

Music-Victor Young

THE OUTLAW

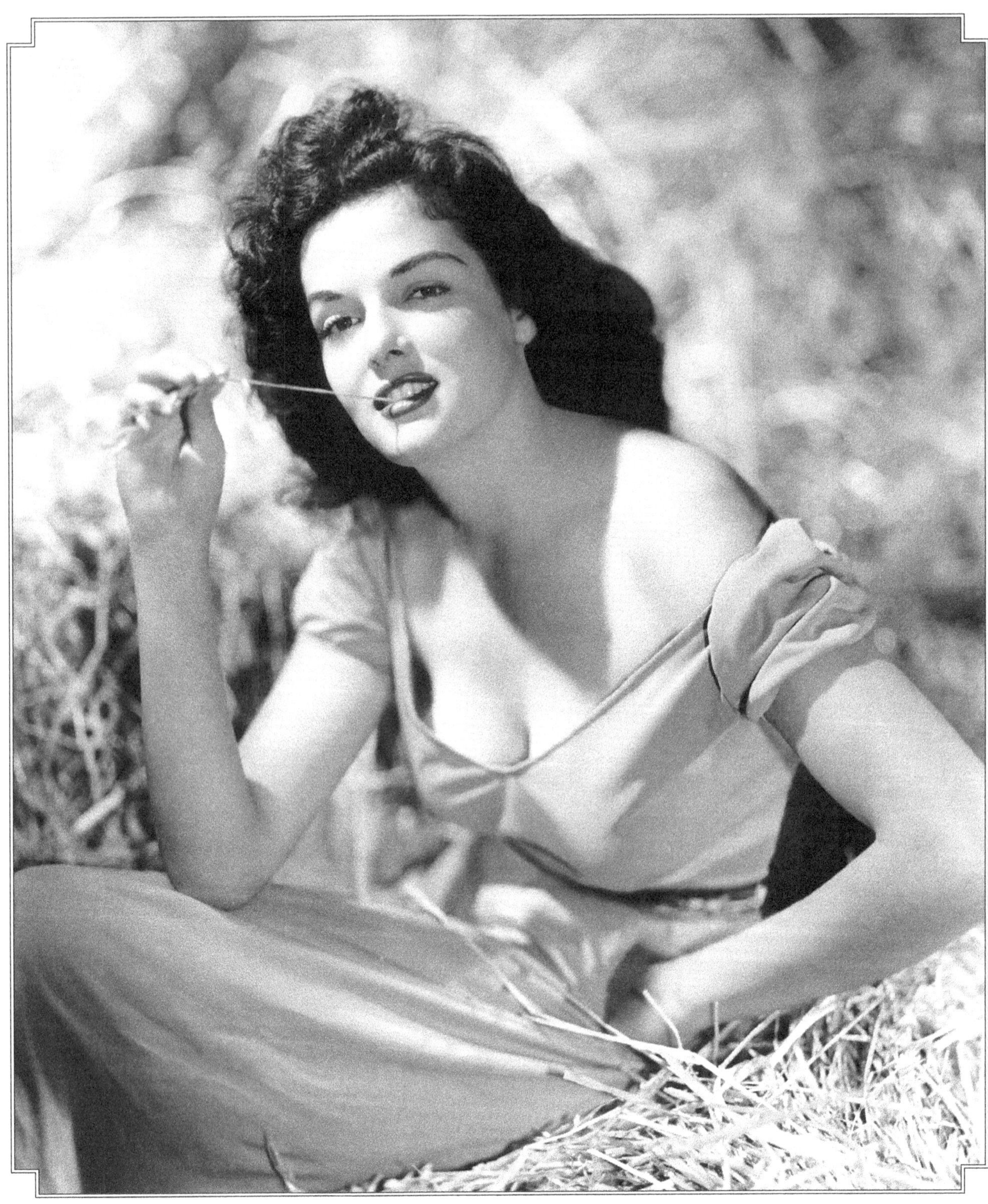

BILLY, YOU MUSN'T. YOU'LL HURT YOURSELF.

Jane Russell as Rio

Jack Buetel as Billy the Kid

Walter Huston as Doc Holiday

This film actually finished production in 1941 but was not released full scale until 1948. This was all because Howard Hughes couldn't get a seal of approval from the Breen office. (The Breen office was the censorship office of the Golden Age of Hollywood.) The problem was a high voltage scene where Jane takes off part of her clothes to warm up a sick Billy the Kid. The scene was finally excised yet the film was still considered controversial.

The film was really about a stolen horse, and it introduced to the world, a beautiful, young, voluptuous brunette. A natural beauty with gorgeous black hair, long, long legs and a pouty, sultry attitude. Jane Russell plays Rio.

> Walter Huston is Doc Holiday, Rio's boyfriend. He brings a wounded Billy the Kid to Rio's house. She'll hide him and tend to his wounds.
>
> At first, she wants to kill him then decides to nurse him back to good health. She heats some big stones and puts them near his feet to warm him. Then she says these famous lines, "You're not gonna die. I'll get you warm." She starts to take off her blouse. End of scene.

And that's how Billy the Kid really got well. I don't care what the history books say. Howard Hughes wouldn't lie to us!

Jane did much to create a market for low-cut blouses and nearly put hospitals out of business with her modern technology for curing pneumonia. Let's hear it for Jane! Jane Russell developed into a major box-office star-acting, singing, dancing, and wise-cracking her way through a lot of films. She was always popular with co-stars and crews. See! Nice does finish first!

RKO-1948

Black and White

Producer/Director-Howard Hughes

Musical Score-Victor Young

Cinematography-Greg Tolland

A LETTER TO THREE WIVES

ANYBODY WANTS ME CAN COME IN AND GET ME, THIS AIN'T A DRIVE-IN. (Lora Mae says these words!)

Linda Darnell as Lora Mae Finney

Paul Douglas as Porter Hollingsworth

Talk about being from the wrong side of the tracks. Lora Mae is.

> This house is so close to the tracks that when the train races by, the house literally shakes, doors open, dishes clatter and everyone stops doing anything.
>
> First date: Lora Mae is ready to be picked up by Porter. He honks the horn. She doesn't move. He rings the doorbell and comes in. This is the way she wants to be treated. She won't settle for less. And so begins her program to train Porter and to seduce him.
>
> After the date, he drives her up to a romantic spot. Moonlight on the water, etc. She's having none of it. He's irritated and drives her home. She's playing him like a piano! He opens the door on her side to let her out. And she has a run in her stocking. She flashes some gorgeous legs. His eyes pop. His throat is dry. She goes into the house and leaves him standing at the door partially paralyzed.
>
> Over a series of dates, Lora seduces Porter, and he doesn't even know it. Fleeting touches and kisses. Those beautiful, seductive eyes of Linda's but NO sex. She wants a wedding ring, nothing less. He's frightened of the commitment. She insists on it.
>
> They part.
>
> It's New Year's Eve and she's at home-her sister is just leaving. The doorbell rings. It's Porter. He wants to take her to a fancy party. She says no. This is going nowhere. He's crazy about her and finally says he'll marry her, not the most romantic proposal, but she'll take it.

Through this entire pursuit, all we've ever seen is a little smooching, lots of Linda's gorgeous gams and a GREAT DEAL OF TALENT. Plus, sparkling dialogue like "WHAT I GOT DON'T NEED BEADS."

20th Century Fox-1949

Black and White

Director-Joseph Mankiewicz

Music-Alfred Newman

Cinematography-Arthur Miller

Costume Design-Kay Nelson

SAMSON AND DELILAH

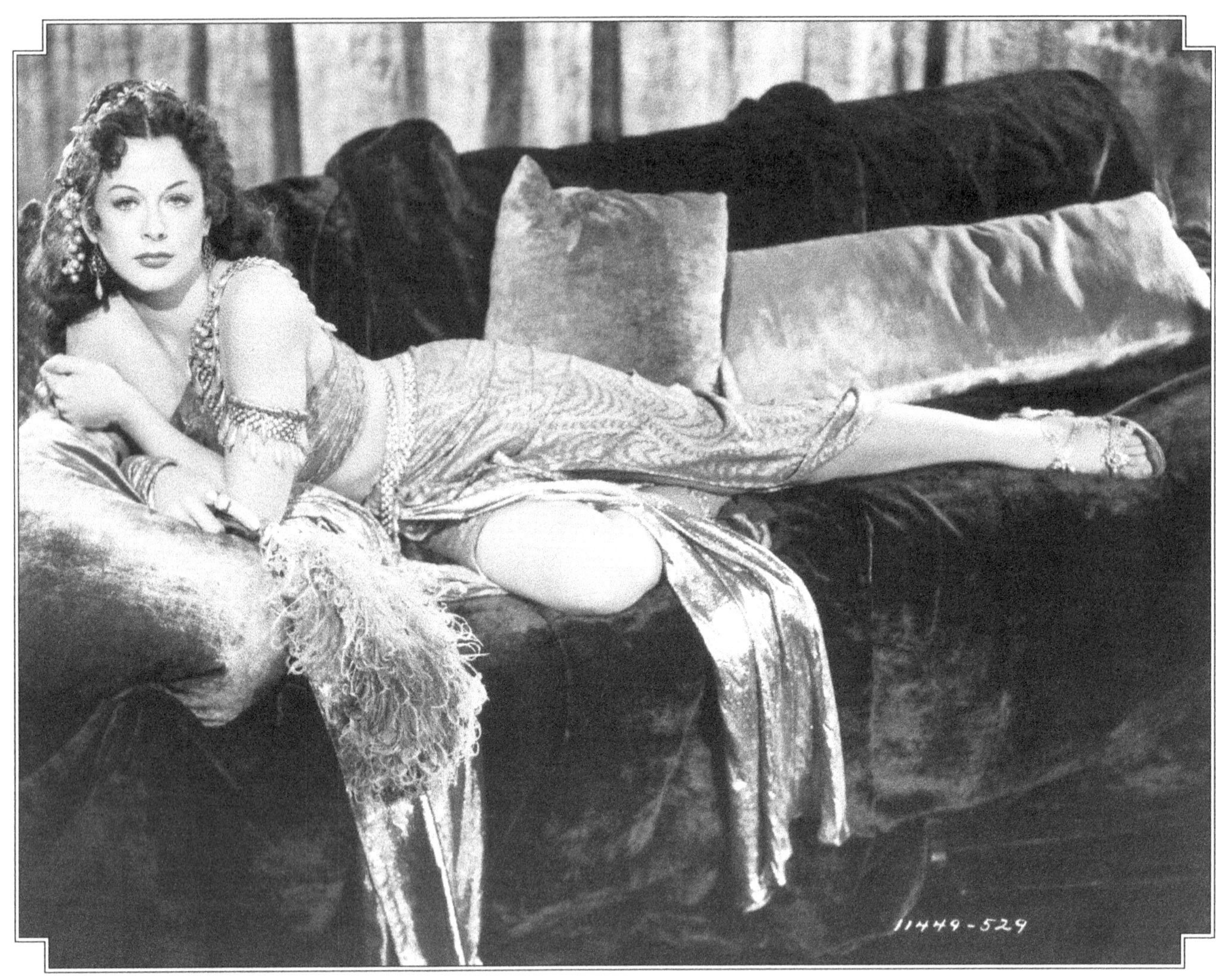

IF YOU CRUSH THE LIFE OUT OF ME, I'D KISS YOU WITH MY DYING BREATH.

Hedy Lamar as Delilah

Victor Mature as Samson

George Saunders as Lord Saran

"If you crush the life out of me, I'd kiss you with my dying breath." Delilah uttered these words to Samson before the wedding feast turned into carnage and her father and sister were both killed.

She has just made a deal with Lord Saran and his generals to capture Samson.

Delilah said, "I will deliver Samson to you before the month of the harvest."

They'll grab at any straw. Samson is a terrible thorn in their side.

It's daytime. Samson and his men are hiding in the hills, striking terror at the troops down below, then returning to the hills where it's impossible to catch them. He looks down to see a caravan winding its way along the route. "A Philistine plum ripe to pick." It's Delilah's caravan!

She camps by an oasis and dismisses the troops. She knows he will strike; she waits for him. He doesn't fail her. He sneaks into the tent and looks for, and finds, some treasure. Seeing her behind the gauze curtains, he asks, why is she here?

Delilah answers, "I'm expecting a caller."

Samson asks, "Who?"

"You, Samson."

He realizes that it is Delilah.

Delilah became known as the world's most famous seductress. Even today, grown men get on their camel and get out of town when they hear that Delilah has arrived!

Paramount Pictures-1949

Director-Cecil B. DeMille

Screenplay-Jesse Lasky & Frederic M. Frank

Cinematography-George Barnes

Costume Design-Edith Head, Dorothy Jeakins, Elois W. Jenssen

A PLACE IN THE SUN

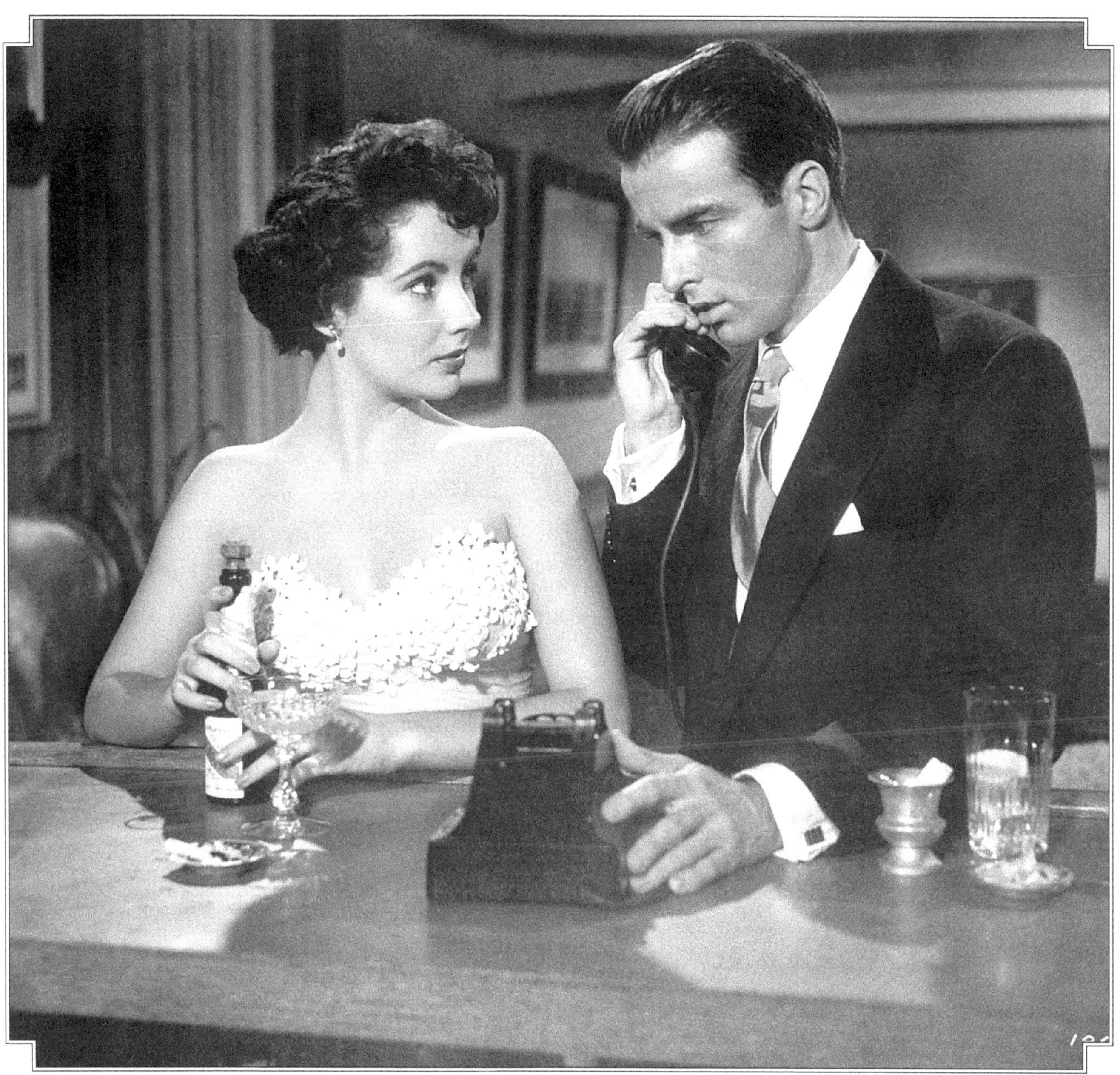

A PLACE IN THE SUN

GOODBYE, GEORGE—SEEMS LIKE WE ALWAYS SPEND THE BEST PART OF OUR TIME JUST SAYING GOODBYE.

Montgomery Clift as George Eastman

Elizabeth Taylor as Angela Vickers

Shelley Winters as Alice Tripp

George Eastman has just come into town hoping to get a job at his uncle's swimsuit factory. His uncle arranges it. The first day, he's put on the end of a conveyor belt, stacking boxes.

A few feet away, wrapping and packing boxes is Alice. She's a rather plain girl. They immediately connect, possibly sensing each other's loneliness. There is a company policy about employees mixing, so they begin to see each other on the sly.

They've just come home from dinner. It's pouring outside.

They get out of the car and make a run for it. They huddle under the overhang outside her window. He kisses her.

Alice says, "Gee, I wish I could invite you in, but Mrs. Roberts is so strict."

George responds, "I don't want to make things difficult for you."

He reaches in through the open window and turns the radio on. It's too loud! He runs up the steps into the room and turns the radio down. Now he's inside her apartment. She's still outdoors.

He teases her, "Yeah, I wish I could ask you in, but we'll have to keep the music low!"

Alice comes in. He takes her in his arms and begins to dance slowly. No lights are on except streetlights. We can barely make out the figures. The rain is still coming down in torrents. The radio is playing mambo music.

George says, "This is nice."

Alice says hushed, "Mrs. Roberts is right next door."

"This is the way it should have been."

Alice again, "George. Oh, George."

We see a close shot of the radio still playing; a curtain of rain blurring everything.

It's morning. We hear static from the radio. The rain has stopped and through the window we see George going down the steps quietly. We don't want to disturb Mrs. Roberts!

All the while he's romancing Alice, he's thinking of Angela. He's seen her several times. She never notices him. He, on the other hand, has fallen in love with a dream.

His uncle invites him to a fancy party. George arrives. No one acknowledges him. He quietly fades away, finds a pool table, and begins to kill some time. Then, she comes in!! Angela is absolutely ethereal.

She's attracted to him - his openness and his honesty.

They go into the ballroom and dance for hours. His dream has become a reality. The close-ups are exquisite when they dance. They make plans.

Just seeing her was a form of seduction. Their romance is perfect, until he makes a fatal mistake, all in the name of love.

Elizabeth Taylor said that this was her first important movie as an adult. The casting is perfect. They had great chemistry between them. And they remained great, personal friends until he died.

How's that for taste and class and PERFECTION?

Paramount-1951

Black and White

Producer/Director-George Stevens

Novel-Theodore Dreiser

Score-Franz Waxman

Costume Design-Edith Head

A PLACE IN THE SUN

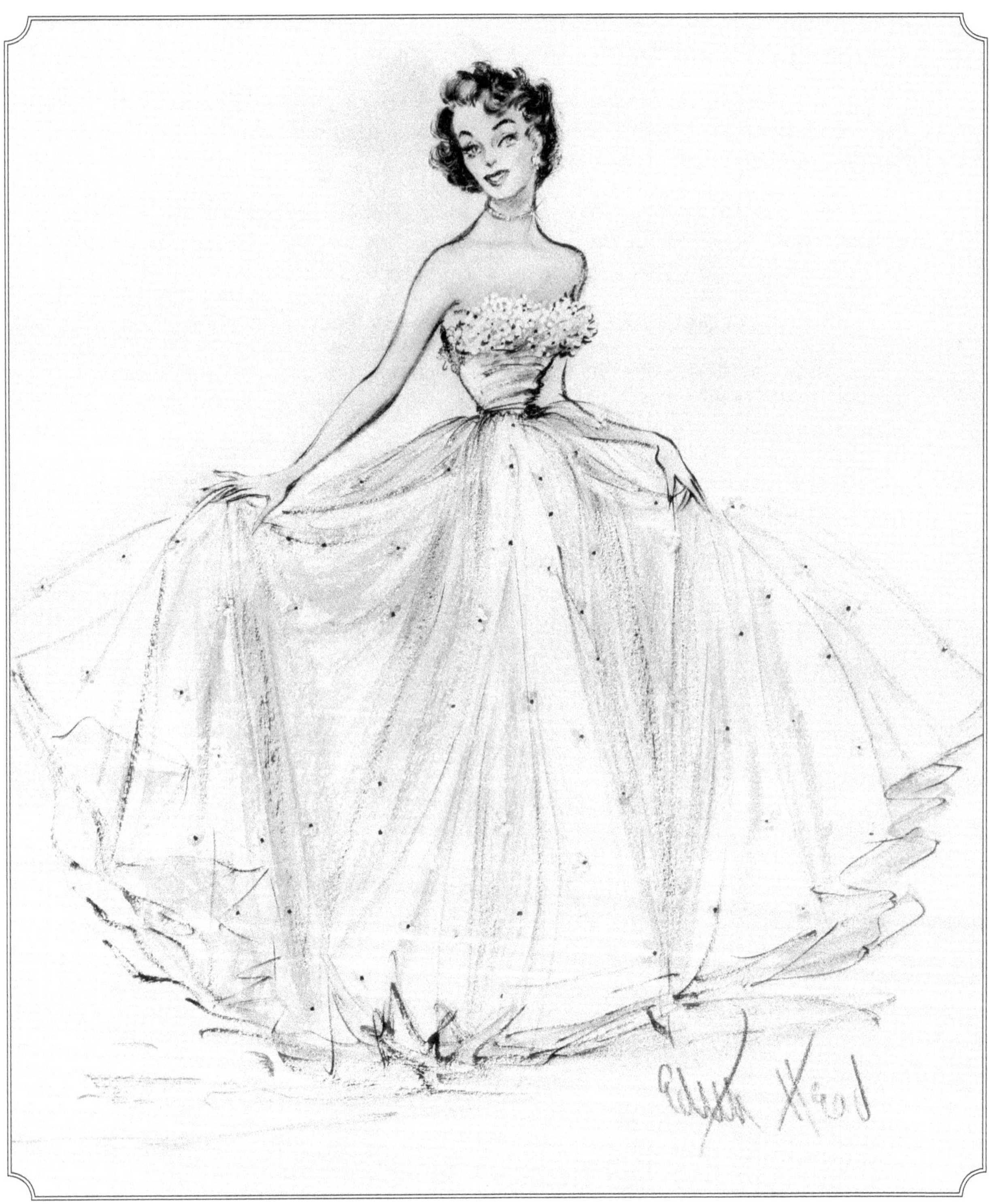

Edith Head won the Academy Award for costumes in a black and white film for this dress worn by Elizabeth Taylor.

THE QUIET MAN

HAVEN'T I BEEN TRYIN' TO TELL YA? THAT UNTIL YOU HAVE MY DOWRY, YOU HAVEN'T GOT ANY BIT OF ME-ME, MYSELF.

John Wayne as Sean Thronton

Maureen O'Hara as Mary Kate

Victor McLaughlin as Mary Kate's brother, Squire 'Red' Will Danaher

Barry Fitzgerald as Flynn, the Matchmaker

Sean has just returned from America to the village in Ireland where he was born. He was a boxer, killed a man in the ring, and vowed never to fight again.

He arrives on the train, gets off, and waits for his ride to the village. Finally, Flynn arrives. They get in the carriage and we're on our way.

Then his life is changed! From the moment that he sees Mary Kate tending the sheep in the field, her red hair a-flyin', he's in love. Mary Kate leads him on a merry chase! And what a chase it is, over green hills and through brooks. This is a virtual travelogue of Ireland, lush and green, and full of tradition. She marries him but will not give herself to him until her brother gives them her dowry. The brother is a bully and a man of importance in the village.

Sean takes as much abuse as he can, from Mary Kate and from her brother. This leads to one of the longest fights in film history. The men end the fight through sheer exhaustion and return to Sean's house. Mary Kate knows she'll "be getting her dowry" now.

Now Sean is welcome in his own bed. A few days later, they're out by the fence watching the same brother begin the courting process they had just been through. They laugh and head back to the house.

Mary Kate whispers something in Sean's ear. He laughs and they continue their walk.

No one knows what she said, but I'll bet it had nothing to do with leprechauns or four-leaf clovers! This was one of the biggest money makers Republic Pictures ever had. John Ford put a lot of his

Irish cronies to work-those charmin' rascals! In glorious Technicolor, this film was one of the "Duke's" favorites, and Maureen starred with him in several other films.

Republic Pictures-1952

Technicolor

Director-John Ford

Musical Score-Victor Young

Costume Design-Adele Palmer

Cinematography-Winton C. Hoch

FROM HERE TO ETERNITY

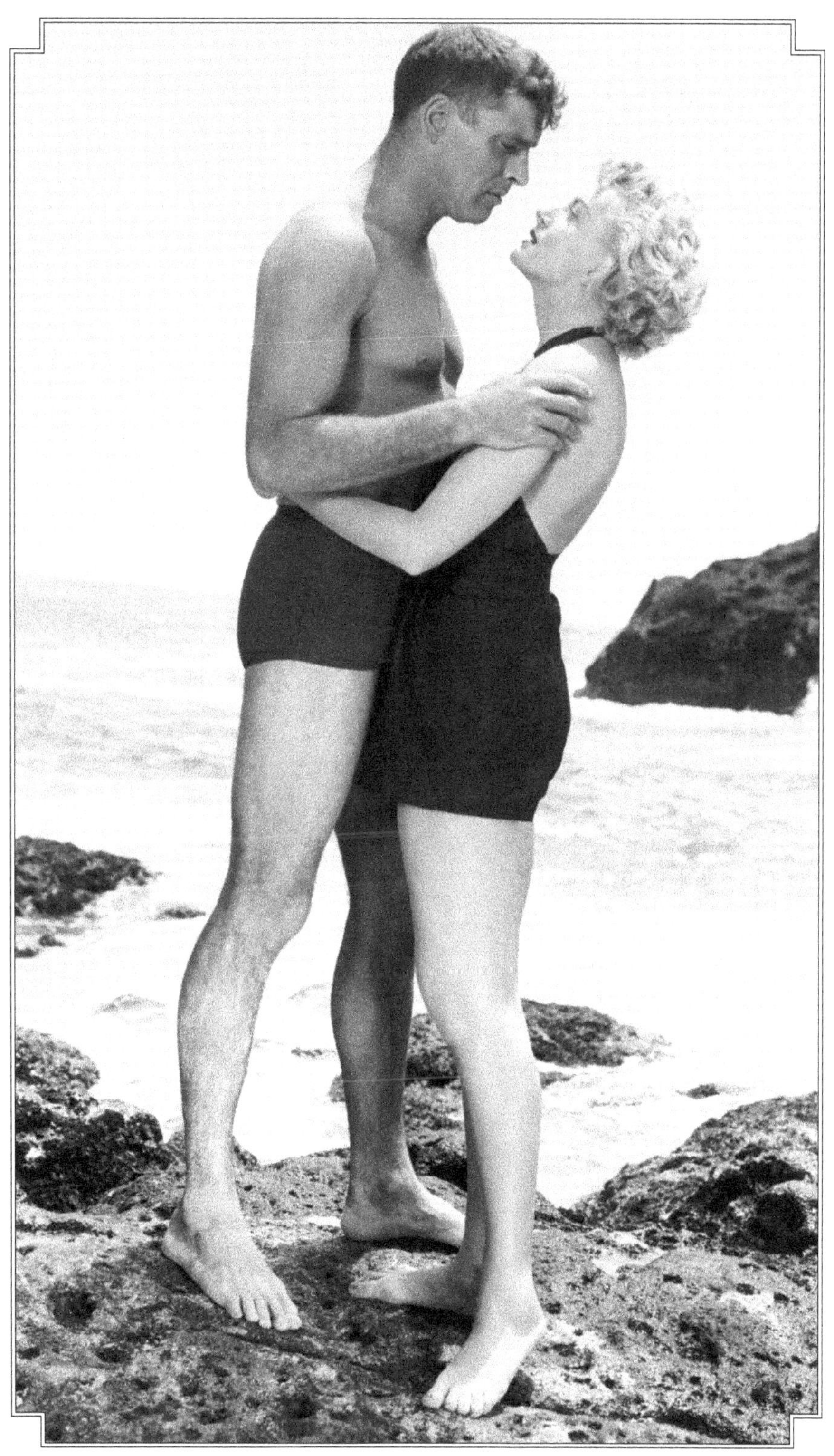

FROM HERE TO ETERNITY

FROM HERE TO ETERNITY

I JUST HATE TO SEE A BEAUTIFUL WOMAN GO TO WASTE.

Deborah Kerr as Karen Holmes, the Captain's Wife

Burt Lancaster as Sgt. Milton Warden

Montgomery Clift, Frank Sinatra, Donna Reed, and **Ernest Borgnine**

It's 1941, just prior to Pearl Harbor. U.S. Army base in Hawaii. Burt Lancaster is the Captain's right-hand man-even covering for his drinking and extramarital affairs. The Captain's marriage has gone sour, but divorce is taboo for a career man in the service. Karen Holmes knows he's unfaithful. She's trapped.

The Warden goes to the Captain's quarters to have some papers signed. He's out. But she's in, wearing a short sleeve blouse and shorts. They banter back and forth. She's sullen, humiliated as everyone knows of their marital problems. They talk. She softens.

Warden asks, "Are you going to cry?"

Karen says, "Not if I can help it. What are you doing?"

"I'm leaving. Isn't that what you want?"

"I don't know, Sergeant, I don't know."

He comes back from the door. He takes her in his arms and tenderly kisses her. Now we're outside looking through the window, rain slamming onto the panes. They're still in that embrace.

First Date: And one of the most famous love scenes in film history! It's night. They're on the beach, both in swimsuits. They run into the water splashing like children. Karen runs out of the water, falls onto the sand. He falls on top of her for a long, long kiss, the sea washing over them. She gets up, runs toward the blanket, and falls down exhilarated. He follows, bends over her, and kisses her.

Karen says, "I never knew it could be like this. No one ever kissed me the way you do."

He says, "Nobody?" (Jealousy creeping in.)

"Nobody!"

"Not even one, not of all the men you've been kissed by?" He's being childish, mean. They quarrel. She runs, he grabs her.

She tells him about the unhappy marriage, the loss of the baby. He's ashamed. He holds her. The waves crash a lot!

Columbia Pictures-1953

Director-Fred Zinnemann

Screenplay-Daniel Taradash

Novel-James Jones

Costume Design-Jean Louis

Cinematographer-Burnett Guffey

CARMEN JONES

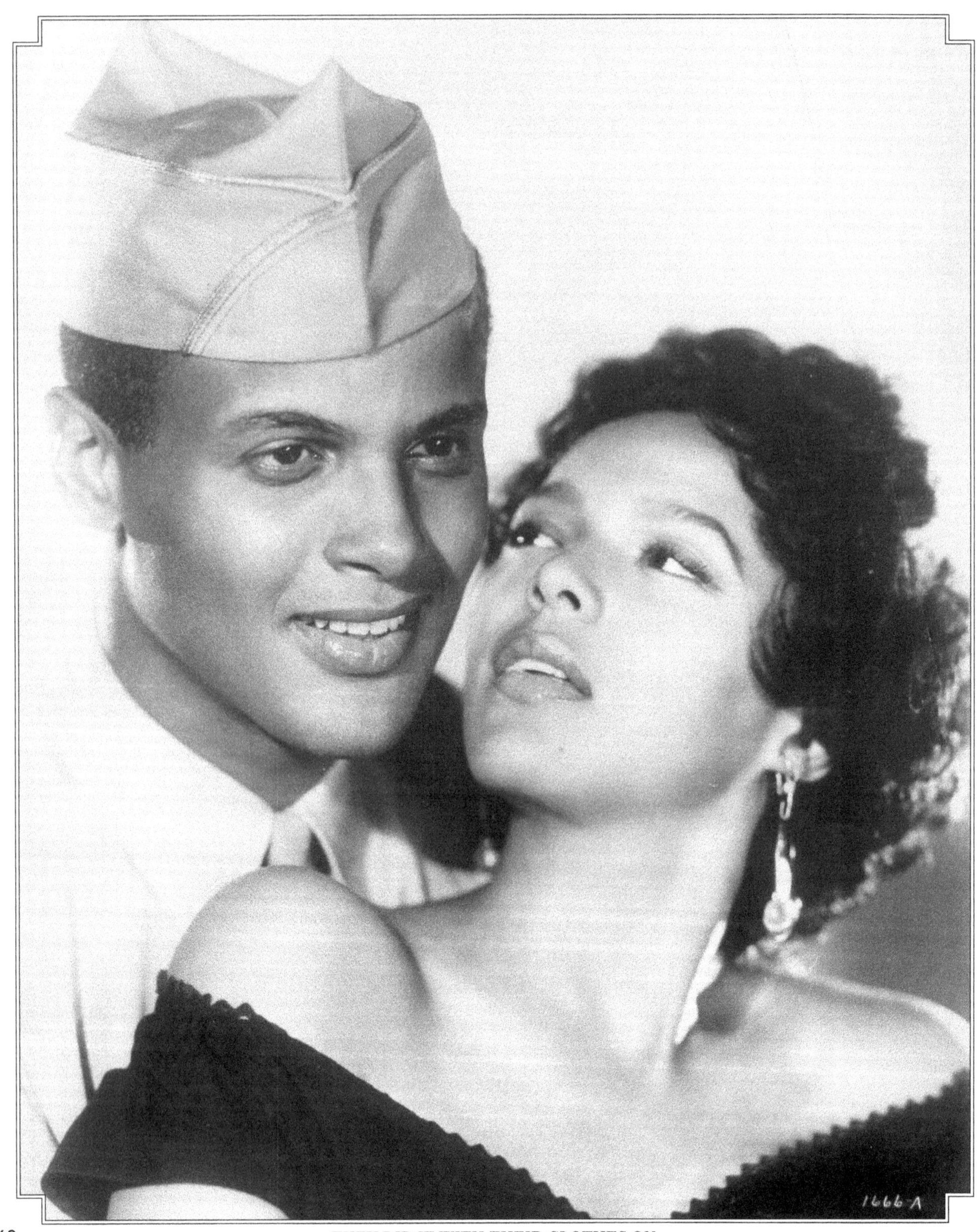

THE WINDS BLOW IN ANOTHER DIRECTION AND I DON'T ARGUE WITH THE WIND.

Harry Belafonte as Joe, The Army Corporal

Dorothy Dandridge as Carmen Jones

This is a modern version of Bizet's opera *CARMEN*, circa World War II. The locale was moved from a cigarette factory to a government parachute factory.

> Carmen first meets Joe in the cafeteria. He's with his sweetheart. Carmen does not care. She flirts outrageously-sassy, funny, sensuous. This girl is trouble-in-a-red-shirt!
>
> Later, she's arrested when caught fighting with another girl. The Sergeant picks Joe to take her to Masonville to a civilian jail. In the jeep, and on the road, she's all over him. He resists her as best as he can. She's having fun with him!
>
> They come to a fork in the road; he makes the wrong choice, and the jeep ends up stuck in the creek. He can't move it. She talks him into walking into town. This is "Carmen Territory." Everyone knows Carmen. They pick up food, including some fresh peaches. She's "gonna fix" him a dinner "he won't forget."
>
> They find their way to Grandma's house. She starts to cook dinner, brushes the dried mud off his pants, and shines his shoes. This is a busy girl. Her career could have gone several ways! Then she notices his belt is twisted in the back. He turns around to fix it, instead she undoes the buckle and pulls the belt out of the loops. Are you following this? He's numb while this is taking place.
>
> Carmen asks, "What's the matter? Don't you trust me, huh? Or don't you trust yourself?"
>
> He kisses her. She takes the peach out of his hand, throws it back over her shoulder. It splatters on the wall, part of it sticking. He kisses her again.

That's all, folks. This gorgeous, brazen hussy has become his undoing. What a dazzling role!

20th Century Fox-1954

Technicolor

Director-Otto Preminger

Script-Oscar Hammerstein, Harry Kleiner

Cinematography-Sam Leavitt

Costume Design-Mary Ann Nyberg

TO CATCH A THIEF

HOLD THIS NECKLACE IN YOUR HAND AND TELL ME YOU'RE NOT JOHN ROBIE, THE CAT.

Cary Grant as John Robie, the cat burglar

Grace Kelly as Francie Stevens

And the beauty of the French Riviera all brought to us by Alfred Hitchcock.

Cary Grant is the retired, infamous "Cat Burglar." He gave it all up to fight in the resistance, World War II, and now there's a copy-cat burglar. The French Police think it's him. He's trying to trap the burglar with the aid of an insurance investigator who has a list of wealthy tourists. They plan on watching these tourists in case the new "Cat" shows up. Two of the tourists that he's watching are a wealthy American, Grace Kelly, and her mother, Jessie Royce Landis (who is a treat)!

Francie invites John up to her suite for dinner. He can't as he's going to watch the fireworks. She tells him that if he doesn't join her, she'll tell the police who he really is. And, really, the view of the fireworks is even better from her suite! He changes his mind. He arrives dressed in a tuxedo, elegant as you'd expect. She's in a gorgeous white, strapless gown with diamonds glittering around her neck. Really breathtaking. And she's right, the view is better from her suite.

They banter back and forth. She actually wants to join him in his next caper. She's totally enamored of him and believes that he's doing the burglaries.

She sits down…

Francie says, "Give up, John. Admit who you are. Even in this light I can tell where your eyes are looking."

He sits next to her on the beautiful Louie-the-something couch.

"Look, John. Hold them. Diamonds. Only thing in the world you can't resist. Then tell me I don't know what I'm talking about."

Beautiful shot of the fireworks. Many colors exploding, falling, dancing in all directions. She kisses his fingertips.

She adds, "Ever had a better offer in your whole life? One with everything?"

He answers, “I’ve never had a crazier one.”

“Just as long as you’re satisfied.”

John says, “You know the necklace is imitation as well as I do.”

Francie says, “BUT I’M NOT.”

He kisses her and we see a lingering shot of fireworks.

Paramount Pictures-1955

Technicolor

Director-Alfred Hitchcock

Cinematography-Robert Burks

Costume Design-Edith Head

PICNIC

THERE COMES A TIME IN A MAN'S LIFE WHEN HE HAS TO QUIT ROLLIN' AROUND LIKE A PINBALL.

William Holden as Hal, the drifter

Kim Novak as Madge, the town beauty

It's summertime. Everyone's at the lake. The picnic is over. It's evening. Chinese lanterns are everywhere, casting wonderful reflections on the water.

The band starts to play "Moonglow" and "Picnic," intertwining the melodies. Romantic. Hal is already on the dance floor. Madge is at the top of the steps. You can feel his throat tighten when he sees her. She's gorgeous. She dances down the steps toward him. They start to dance separately. Then their hands reach out and touch. Time stands still. Dancing apart, moving closer together, slowly.

Their eyes never leave each other. Dancing, barely moving, they know this is love! We know this is love! The song ends (and not a moment too soon.)

Late that night, there's trouble at the dance. Hal is blamed and jumps into a car. Madge follows him and gets into the car. They drive out by the railroad tracks and get out of the car. He spills his heart out about his past, time in jail, drifting from town to town, never belonging. He's going to hop on a freight train. Madge literally throws herself on him and kisses him passionately. He's stunned!

Hal says, "Baby, what'd you do?"

Madge answers, "I get so tired just being told I'm pretty."

They kiss. She moves away and stumbles. Hal follows her.

She says, "The others. We've got to get back to the picnic."

"Do we?"

He holds her. The freight train that he was going to hop on is going by. It's a long train and he's not moving. He's still holding her.

Meanwhile the harvest moon is doing its best to help. It's letting those pesky clouds hide its light, for a while.

After all, there's only so much that a moon can do!

Columbia Pictures-1955

Technicolor

Director-Josh Logan

Play-William Inge

Cinematography-James Wong Howe

Costume Design-Jean Louis

TEA AND SYMPATHY

YEARS FROM NOW, WHEN YOU TALK ABOUT THIS, AND YOU WILL, BE KIND.

Deborah Kerr as Laura Reynolds

John Kerr (no relation) as Tom

Lief Erickson as Laura's husband, Bill Reynolds

Tom is a young college student, insecure, sensitive, with a definite crush on his house master's wife. Laura is that older woman, about forty, gentle, understanding, beautiful, and living in a rather loveless marriage to a man who would rather spend time with the male students than with her. Also, he is too insensitive to see that Tom just needs a little understanding. And Tom gets that understanding from Laura.

This rainy night, all dressed up to go meet the town tart and a little drunk, Tom passes Laura's quarters and goes in. She attempts to sober him up. Minutes pass. He grabs her, kisses her, and then begins to cry, full of terrible despair.

He goes to his original date's apartment. She tries to seduce him. He cracks, grabs a kitchen knife, and attempts suicide. However, the police intervene.

The next morning, Laura goes to his room and finds several crumpled, unfinished suicide notes. She gets in her car and drives everywhere, looking for him. She finally sees his bicycle by the roadside, parks and runs through the shrubs and finds him lying there.

She goes to him. She's wearing a sweater over her shoulders (buttoned only at the top), a blouse and a skirt.

They talk, he's ashamed of all his actions the previous night.

He's still lying on the ground. He turns away from her, she walks away, turns around, and is unbuttoning that top button of the sweater... That's All!

She cradles his face in her hands and says, "Years from now, when you talk about this, and you will, be kind."

In the next shot, we see the wind softly ruffling the curtains in Tom's dormitory window.

Have we ever seen less done and more said?

Metro-Goldyn-Mayer-1956

Producer-Pandro Berman

Director-Vincent Minelli

Cinematography-John Alton

Original Play-Robert Anderson

Costume Design-Helen Rose

SOME LIKE IT HOT

A REAL MILLIONAIRE WITH A BIG YACHT AND A BIGGER CRUSH ON DAPHNE.

Marilyn Monroe as Sugar

Tony Curtis as Joe, the saxophone player, Josephine, his drag counterpart and "The Millionaire"

Jack Lemmon as Jerry, the base player and Daphne his female counterpart

Joe E. Brown as Osgood, a real millionaire with a big crush on Daphne

It's Chicago, 1929. The two boys are on the lam. They've just witnessed the St. Valentine's Day Massacre. They gotta get out of town fast, so they join an all-girl band headed for Florida. They meet the rest of the band at the train station. To see these two guys, dressed as girls, all decked out from the tops of their heads to their weak little ankles, is about as good as it gets!

And we see Sugar hurrying as she's late, of course. (Marilyn is more voluptuous than usual. She's really something to see!) When Joe first sees her, he nearly chews all his lipstick off. He wants her. But he can't have her as Joe, or Josephine, so he invents "The Millionaire" with a yachting cap, glasses, a navy-blue blazer, white pants, and he does a wonderful Cary Grant imitation!

Sugar falls for him, good looking and, for a change, rich! Maybe this time she ends up with money instead of just another saxophone player… maybe not!

Joe steals Osgood's motorboat and takes Sugar aboard the yacht telling her that it's his. He tells her his sad tale of woe. He has a mental block when it comes to women. He had a traumatic shock and it left him unable to make love. Sugar thinks she's just the girl to cure his illness and proceeds to seduce him.

Joe lays down on the couch as though he's there for his therapy session. Sugar turns down the lights, turns on the radio, and all the men in the audience. She dances back to the couch with two glasses of champagne.

Sugar says, "You're not giving yourself a chance. Don't fight it.

Relaaaax." (She kisses him).

Millionaire says, "It's like smoking without inhaling."

"So, inhale." She kisses him. "Well?"

He says, "I'm not quite sure. Would you try it again? I've got a funny sensation in my toes-like someone is barbecuing them on a slow flame."

Sugar says, "Let's throw another log on the fire." Kiss. Kiss.

Millionaire adds, "I think you're on the right track." He's starting to respond.

"I must be. Your glasses are beginning to steam up."

"I never knew it could be like this."

Sugar says, "Thank You."

Millionaire says, "They told me I was kaput-finished-all washed up. And here you are, making a chump out of the experts." She giggles. "Where did you learn to kiss like that?"

Sugar answers, "I used to sell kisses for the milk fund."

"Tomorrow, remind me to send a check for $100,000 to the milk fund."

And his problem is cured. He just needed a little help!!

The Osgood and Daphne Sequence

Osgood says, "I called Mama. She was so happy, she cried. She wants you to have her wedding dress. It's white lace."

Daphne says, "Osgood, I can't get married in your mother's dress. She and I are not built in the same way."

"We can have it altered."

Daphne says, "Oh, no you don't. Osgood, I'm gonna level with you. We can't get married at all."

Osgood asks, "Why not?"

Daphne answers, "Well, in the first place, I'm not a natural blonde."

"It doesn't matter."

"I smoke. I smoke all the time."

Osgood says, "I don't care."

Daphne adds, "Well, I've a terrible past. For the last three years, I've been living with a saxophone player."

Osgood says, "I forgive you."

"I can never have children."

Osgood says, "We can adopt some."

Daphne says, "You don't understand, Osgood." Takes off the wig. "I'm a man."

Osgood, "Well, nobody's perfect."

And the end shot is of Osgood smiling and Jerry muttering to himself. How to get out of this maddening situation? Or maybe, he can picture himself as the mistress of Osgood's mansion! Who knows!

The classic film was shot in 1959 at the beautiful Del Coronado Hotel in San Diego in Black and White. It was directed by Billy Wilder with a great cast and a great musical score.

The beautiful, "Let's Build a Stairway to the Stars" (ah, those lush violins) was the theme for Marilyn and Tony's love scenes.

See you at the Del Coronado and bring a change of clothes. You never know, you might meet a millionaire of some kind!

United Artists-1959

Black and White

Director-Billy Wilder

Cinematographer-Charles Lan, Jr.

Costumes-Orry-Kelly

Score-Adolph Deutch

Song Supervision-Matty Malneck

SPARTACUS

ROME. A TIME OF UNREST. ABOUT ONE HUNDRED YEARS BEFORE THE BIRTH OF CHRISTIANITY.

***Kirk* Douglas** as Spartacus

Jean Simmons as Varinia, the slave girl that he loves

Lawrence Olivier as General Crassus

Tony Curtis as Antonitus a poet, singer of songs and a slave

Crassus is in his bathing pool. He summons Antonitus to fetch a stool and bring it into the pool for him to sit on. The slave helps him bathe.

General Crassus asks, "Do you eat oysters?"

Antonitus answers, "When I have them, master."

General Crassus says, "Do you eat snails?"

"No, master."

General Crassus says, "Of course not. It's all a matter of taste, is it not?

"Yes, master."

General Crassus again, "And taste is not the same as appetite and therefore not a question of morals, is it?"

"It could be agreed so, master."

General Crassus says, "My robe, Antonitus." Getting out of the bath.

Antonitus hands Crassus his robe.

General Crassus adds, "My taste includes both snails and oysters."

Crassus goes to the next room followed by Antonitus. Through an open window we see a magnificent view of Rome.

General Crassus says, "There, boy, is Rome. No man can withstand

Rome. You must love her. Isn't that right, boy?"

He turns to Antonitus. The slave is gone. One of the few maneuvers the General has lost. He stands there smiling.

Spartacus and Varinia have just heard Antonitus sing. He is struck with the knowledge of what he doesn't know, his not being able to read-this thirst for knowledge and peace.

Spartacus says, "I want to know."

Varinia asks, "Know what?"

Spartacus says, "Everything. Why a star falls and a bird doesn't? Where the sun goes at night? Why the moon changes shape? I want to know where the wind comes from?"

Varinia says, "The wind begins in a cave. Far to the north, a young god sleeps in a cave. He dreams of a girl and he sighs. And the night wind stirs his breath." She laughs.

Spartacus says, "I want to know all about you. Every line. Every curve. I want to know every part of you. Every beat of your heart"

He tenderly kisses her.

What poetry!

Universal Picture-1960

Technicolor

Director-Stanley Kubrick

Novel-Howard Fast

Screenplay-Dalton Trumbo

Music-Alex North

Cinematography-Russell Metty

Costume Design-Valles

TOM JONES

WE ARE ALL AS GOD MADE US-AND MANY MUCH WORSE.

Albert Finney as Tom Jones

Joyce Redman as Mrs. Walters

The famous eating scene between Tom Jones and Mrs. Walters was truly a lesson in sexual gymnastics. In fact, it's the last decent movie about sexual excess!

> Our hero is on his way to London, on foot. He reaches the top of a knoll and sees a strange sight. A soldier is attempting to hang a woman, having made a rope out of her blouse. (We never know why he's hanging her.) Tom fights and beats the villain and unties the woman.
>
> One look at her ample bosom and flaming red hair and our hero has fallen into true lust. Her name is Mrs. Walters.
>
> She begs him to be her protector and lead her to the next village. Tom Jones doesn't have the word "no" in his vocabulary, particularly when it comes to females!
>
> They arrive at the inn, he requests food and lodgings and a gown for the lady, no particular color.
>
> Now it's time for dinner. Soup, crab legs: all the time their eyes hardly leave each other, each bite a bit of foreplay. This lady really knows her way around a leg of lamb. Then the oysters, posing and teasing.
>
> This dinner is definitely NOT about food. Now the pears - such biting and chewing like you've never seen on the screen. Are you sure this is legal?
>
> They sip wine, dizzy with expectation. She picks up the candle from the table, literally racing him to her room. He goes to her, snuffs out the flame, the room goes dark.

This bawdy romp made Albert Finney an international film star (and did much to promote candlelight dinners and fluffy beds)!

Woodfall Film Productions-1963

Director-Tony Richardson

Novel-Henry Fielding

Screenplay-John Osborne

Cinematography-Walter Lassally

Costume Design-John McCorry

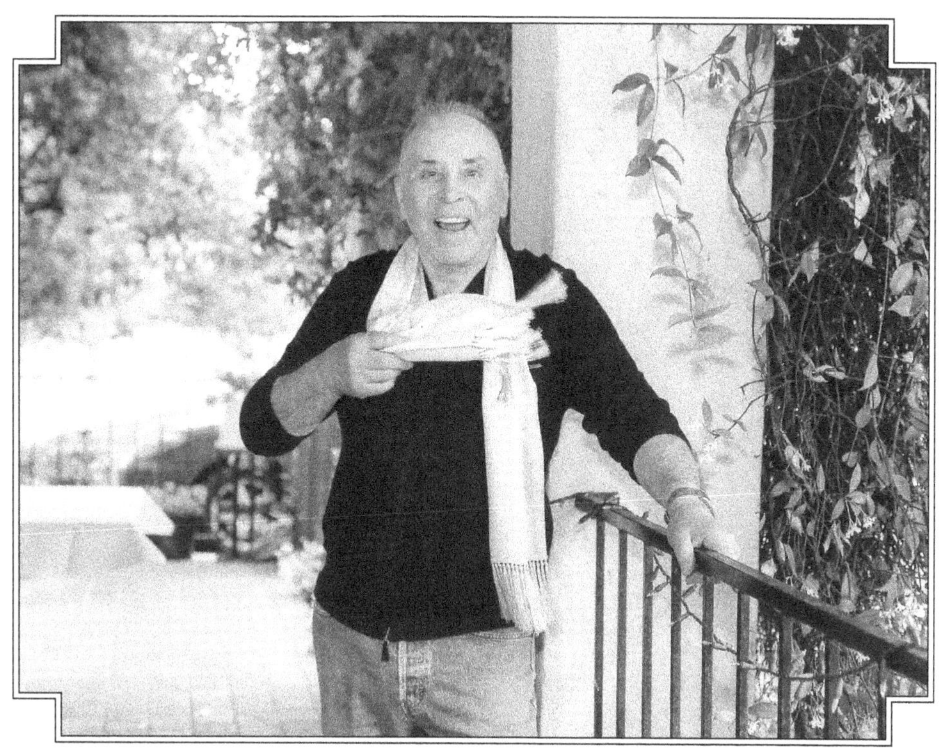

ABOUT THE AUTHOR

This book is a great reminder about "sex and seduction" on the Silver Screen in another time. The stars in these films have shined for a long time. And, yes, they sometimes did it with their clothes on!

Tom Culver resides in Southern California. He had a long film and television career as a Set Costumer.

He worked on many films such as *MOBSTERS* and *TOWN AND COUNTRY* which starred Warren Beatty, Diane Keaton, Gary Shandling and Charlton Heston among others.

He also worked for director Mike Nichols on the film *WHAT PLANET ARE YOU FROM?* which starred Annette Bening and Gary Shandling, to name a few. Tom's television career is just as impressive, working on epic shows like *THE LOVE BOAT* and *MURDER, SHE WROTE*. He is also an author. His first book was a cookbook with recipes from the cast and crew of *MURDER, SHE WROTE*. All the proceeds from the book were donated to the AIDS Foundation. Tom is currently working on his third book, which is about the famous costume designer, Yvonne Wood.

Tom is also a very talented singer and songwriter. Several of Tom's songs have been recorded and had successful airplay. When Tom isn't writing music, books, or singing you'll find him out in the garden with his faithful, four-legged companion, Señor Jack, a beautiful black and white, long-haired cat with an attitude!

Published by

TVGUESTPERT PUBLISHING

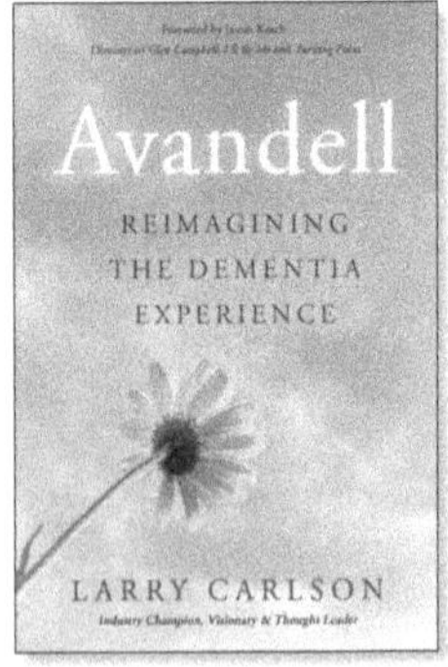

LARRY CARLSON
Avandell: Reimagining the Dementia Experience
Hardcover: $17.95
Kindle: $9.99

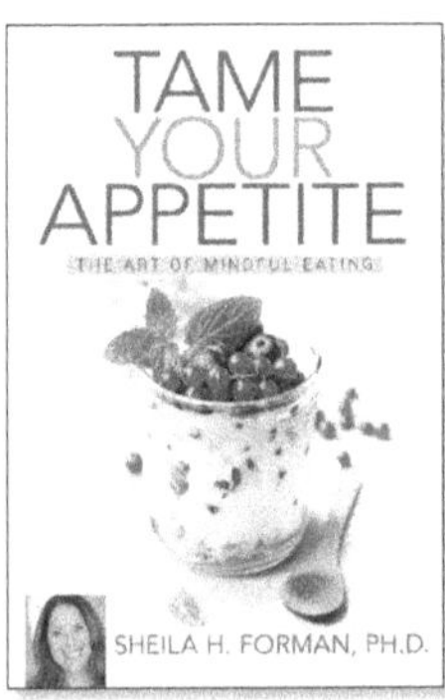

SHEILA H. FORMAN, Ph.D
Tame Your Appetite: The Art of Mindful Eating
Paperback: $16.95
Kindle: $9.99

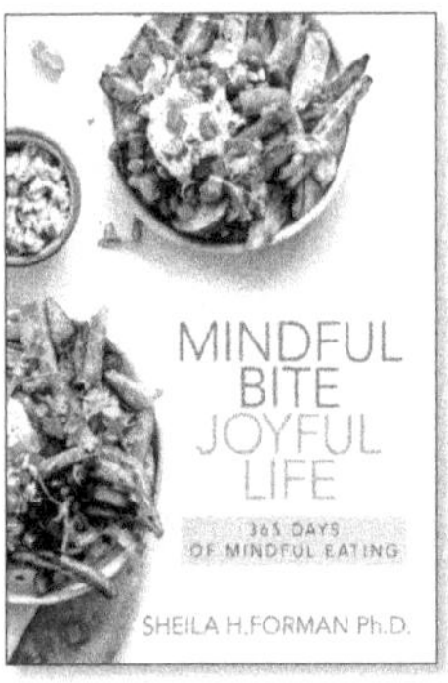

SHEILA H. FORMAN, Ph.D
Mindful Bite, Joyful Life: 365 Days of Mindful Eating
Paperback: $22.95
Kindle: $9.99

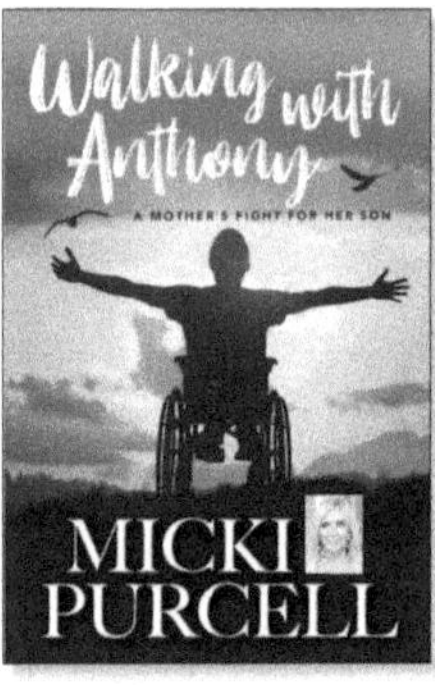

MICKI PURCELL
Walking With Anthony: A Mother's Fight For Her Son
Hardcover $22.95
Kindle: $9.99

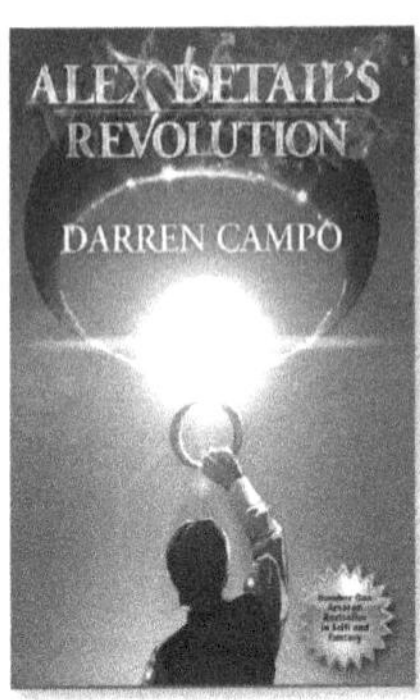

DARREN CAMPO
Alex Detail's Revolution
Paperback: $9.95
Hardcover: $22.95
Kindle: $9.15

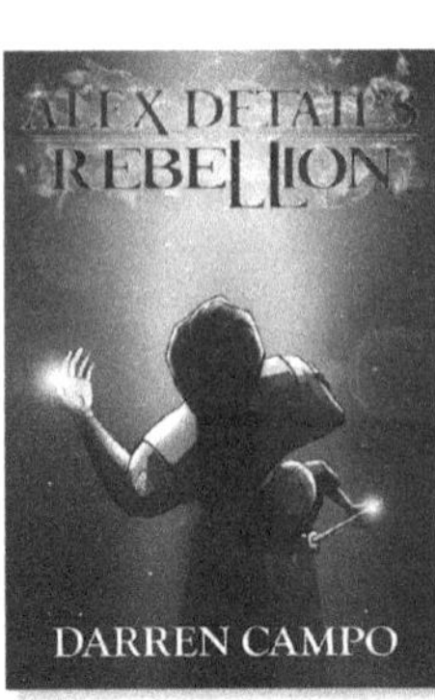

DARREN CAMPO
Alex Detail's Rebellion
Hardcover: $22.95
Kindle: $9.99

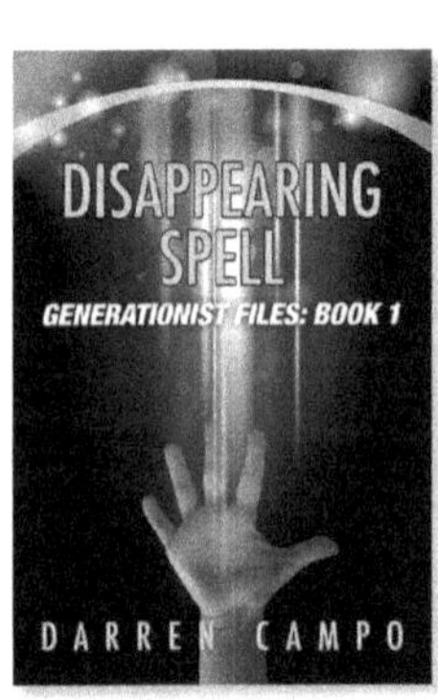

DARREN CAMPO
Disappearing Spell: Generationist Files: Book 1
Kindle: $2.99

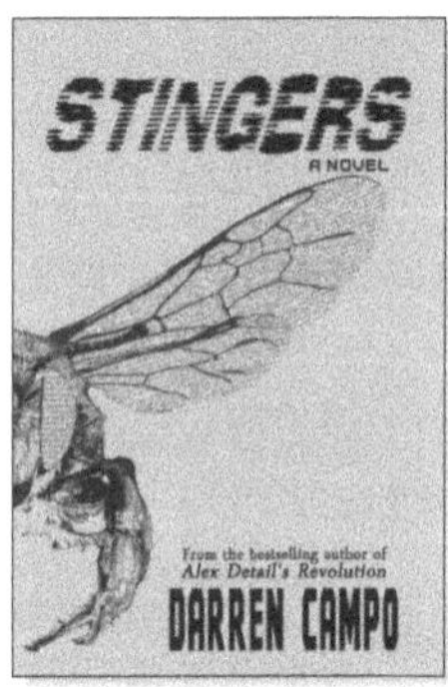

DARREN CAMPO
Stingers
Paperback: $9.99
Kindle: $9.99

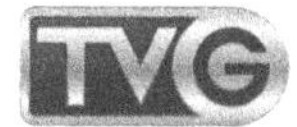

TVGuestpert Publishing
11664 National Blvd, #345
Los Angeles, CA. 90064
310-584-1504
www.TVGPublishing.com

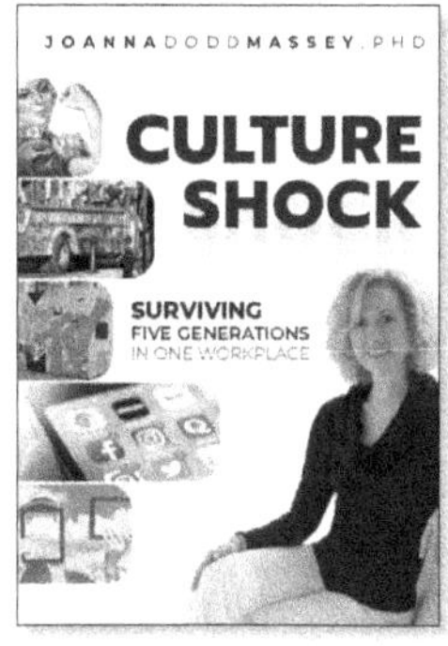

JOANNA DODD MASSEY
Culture Shock: Surviving Five Generations in One Workplace
Paperback: $16.95
Kindle/Nook: $9.99

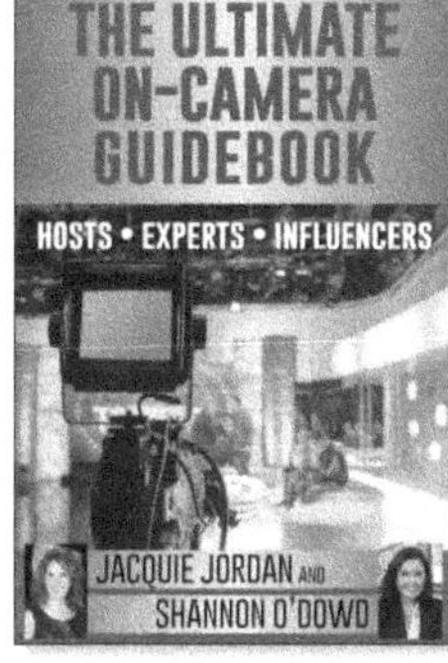

JACQUIE JORDAN AND SHANNON O'DOWD
*The Ultimate On-Camera Guidebook: Hosts*Experts*Influencers*
Paperback: $16.95
Kindle: $9.99

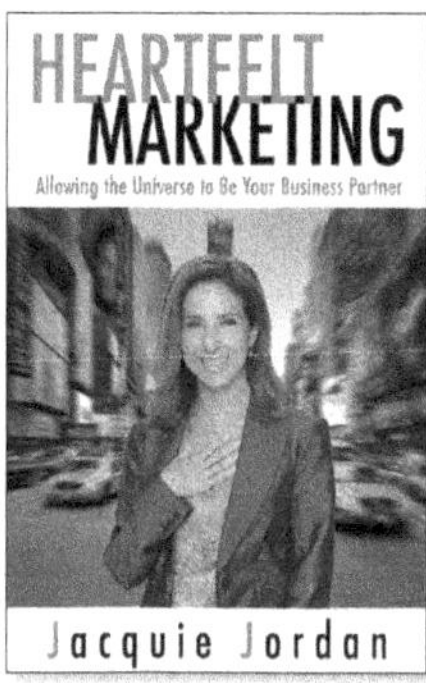

JACQUIE JORDAN
Heartfelt Marketing: Allowing the Universe to Be Your Business Partner
Paperback: $15.95
Kindle: $9.99
Audible: $9.95

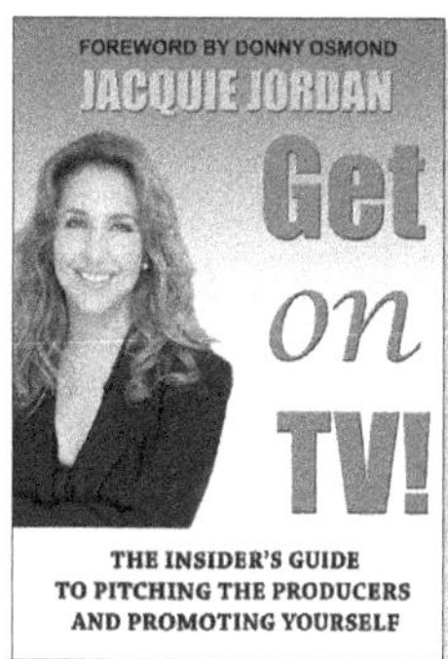

JACQUIE JORDAN
Get on TV! The Insider's Guide to Pitching the Producers and Promoting Yourself
Published by Sourcebooks
Paperback: $14.95
Kindle: $9.99
Nook: $14.95

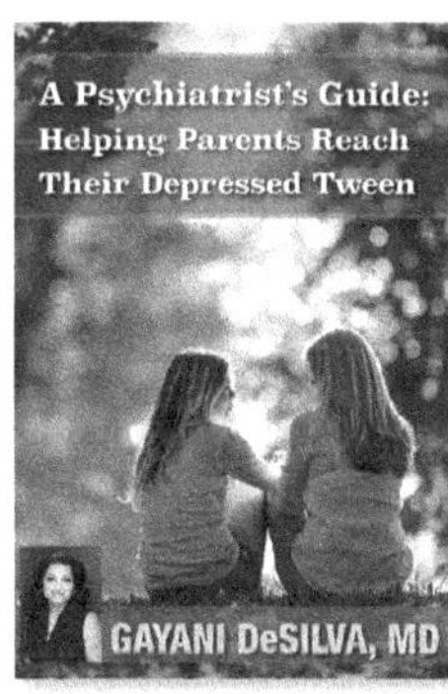

GAYANI DESILVA, MD
A Psychiatrist's Guide: Helping Parents Reach Their Depressed Tween
Paperback: $16.95
Kindle: $9.99

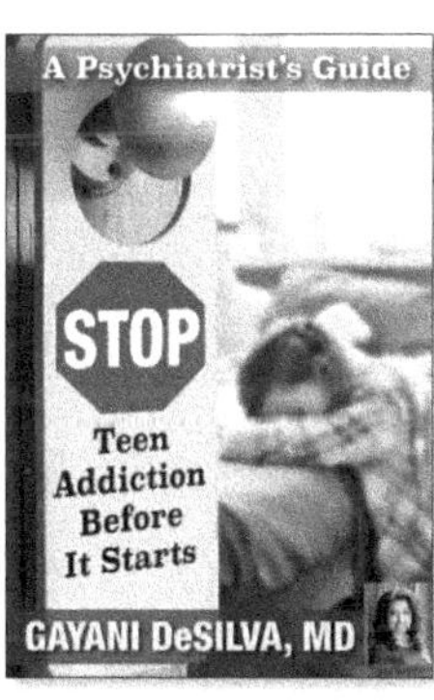

GAYANI DESILVA, MD
A Psychiatrist's Guide: Stop Teen Addiction Before It Starts
Paperback: $16.95
Kindle: $9.99
Audible: $14.95

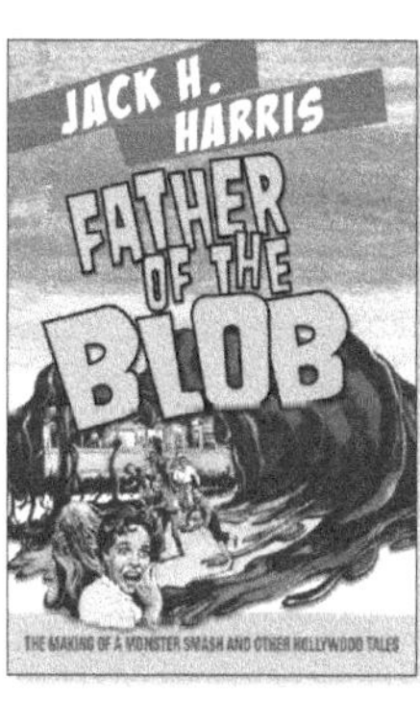

JACK H. HARRIS
Father of the Blob: The Making of a Monster Smash and Other Hollywood Tales
Paperback: $16.95
Kindle/Nook: $9.99

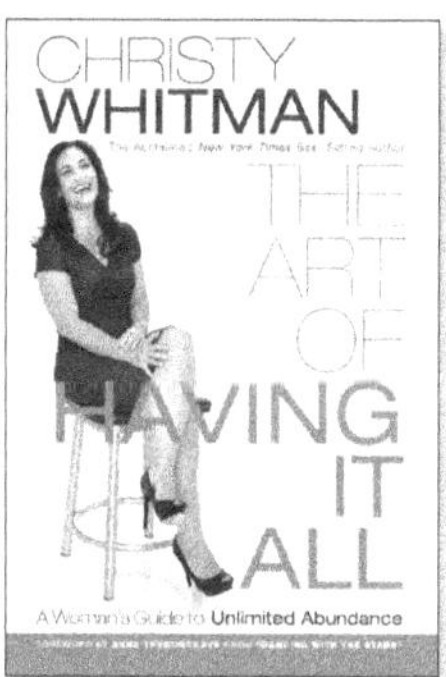

New York Times Best Seller
CHRISTY WHITMAN
The Art of Having It All: A Woman's Guide to Unlimited Abundance
Paperback: $16.95
Kindle/Nook: $9.99
Audible Book: $13.00

Published by

TVGUESTPERT PUBLISHING

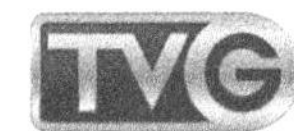

TVGuestpert Publishing
11664 National Blvd, #345
Los Angeles, CA. 90064
310-584-1504
www.TVGPublishing.com

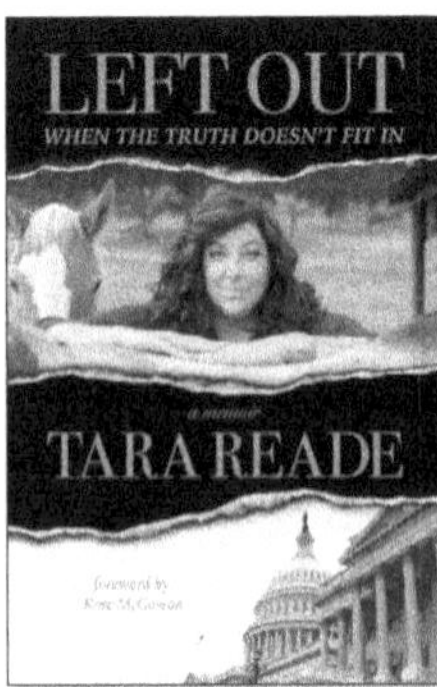

TARA READE
Left Out: When The Truth Doesn't Fit In
Hardcover: $22.95
Paperback: $19.95
Kindle: $9.99

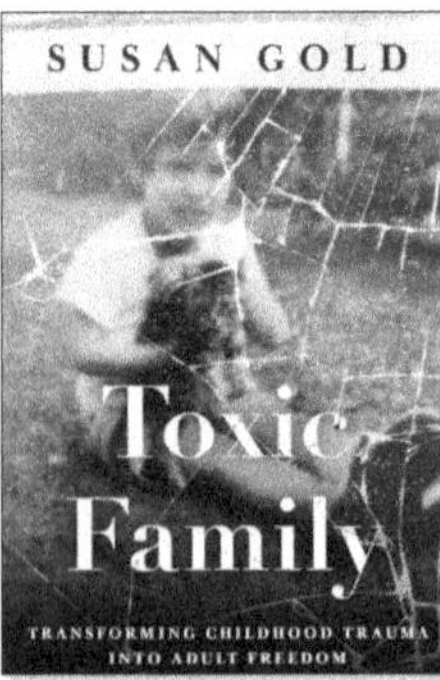

SUSAN GOLD
Toxic Family: Transforming Childhood Trauma into Adult Freedom
Paperback: $19.95
Kindle: $9.99

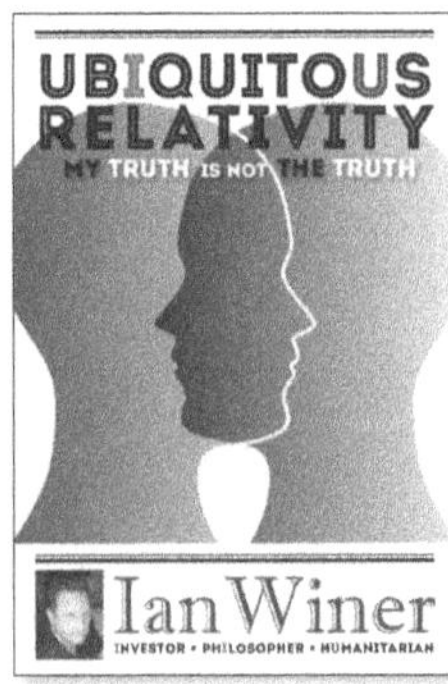

IAN WINER
Ubiquitous Relativity: My Truth is Not the Truth
Paperback: $16.95
Kindle: $9.99

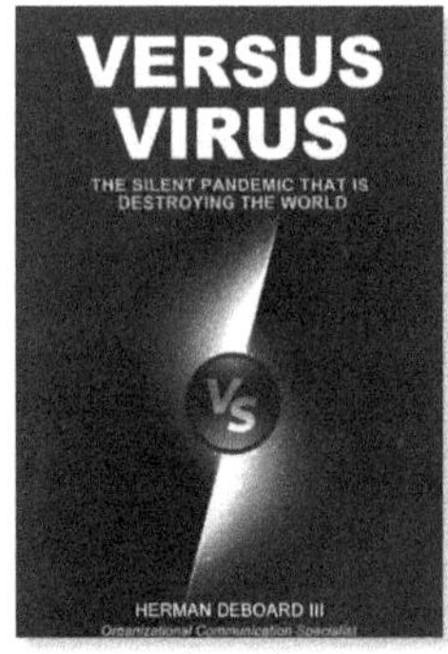

HERMAN DEBOARD III
Versus Virus: The Silent Pandemic That is Destroying the World
Paperback: $9.99

www.ingramcontent.com/pod-product-compliance
Lightning Source LLC
LaVergne TN
LVHW060632110826
845147LV00014B/895
* 9 7 8 1 7 3 5 8 9 8 1 9 3 *